Practical Guide to the Operational Use of the M203 Grenade Launcher

By Erik Lawrence

Copyright ©2014 Erik Lawrence

Erik Lawrence
www.vig-sec.com   erik@vig-sec.com

Printed and bound in the United States of America

First printing 2008
Second printing 2014

ISBN-10: 1-941998-10-0
ISBN-13: 978-1-941998-10-6
EBOOK – ISBN-13: 978-1-941998-29-8
LCCN: Not yet assigned

ATTENTION US MILITARY UNITS, US GOVERNMENT AGENCIES AND PROFESSIONAL ORGANIZATIONS: Quantity discounts are available on bulk purchases of this book. Special books or book excerpts can also be created to fit specific needs. For information, please contact:

Erik Lawrence
www.vig-sec.com   erik@vig-sec.com

SAFETY NOTICE
Before starting an inspection, ensure the weapon is cleared. Do not manipulate the trigger system until the weapon has been cleared of all ammunition. Inspect the chamber to ensure that it is empty and no ammunition is present. Keep the weapon oriented in a safe direction when loading and handling.

AMMUNITION NOTICE - These weapons fire multiple types of grenades, and they must come from trusted sources; never fire captured grenades. Know the capabilities and limitation of each type of grenade. The 40mm grenades used in the M203 (40 x 46 mm) are not the same as in the Mk 19 grenade launcher (40 x 53 mm), which are fired at a higher velocity. Firing the incorrect ammunition will damage the weapon and possibly injure the operator/assistant operator.

Training should be received from knowledgeable and experienced operators on this particular weapons system. Vigilant Security Services, LCCw Training provides this training and continually perfects its instruction with up-to-date information from actual use

www.vig-sec.com

PREFACE

This manual is intended to be a reference for those involved in the use, maintenance and instruction of the featured firearm. My aim in writing these manuals is to set the record straight and dispel many of the false assumptions related to the different firearms. The early sections of the manual contain background material on the featured firearm which allows the user to gain the basic building blocks for further education. The firearms featured in these manuals have been used for decades by our allies and enemies, and will be for the foreseeable future, so why are we not experts with them? If I am fighting with the firearm or providing instruction on a firearm, I want to use and know their system better than they do.

The rationale for writing these manuals comes from the fact that there are not libraries of easily accessible references to use in developing your own training system for these firearms. Many of the old military field manuals are decades old and were incorrectly translated by someone who had no idea what the firearm could do, let alone basic firearm knowledge. We started from the ground up and developed the manuals to provide instruction in progressive steps that could be easily grasped and continually referred back to. A good grounding in the basics of firearms, safety, and instruction allows the user to use these manuals to their maximum value. A competent user will find little difficulty in interpreting and applying the information in the manual to their own training program.

The guide goes through the most fundamental parts of the firearm in detail and more advanced techniques are not covered as extensively. With this in mind the user can use these principles and adapt it as needed to their required level of instruction. The emphasis of this guide is in acquiring familiarity with the fundamentals of all firearms and learned competence rather than becoming a firearms guru.

Many of the points in these guides were developed from scratch in theatres of conflict and are continually improved and updated for each edition. I have continually used vetted points from users and professionals in the guides to continually update them to the best known practices for each particular firearm. If it is valid and relevant we will include it in the next edition.

Please note that this guide assumes some familiarity with the basic concepts in firearm safety, gun handling skills, common sense and an ability to process new information. Readers should have knowledge of the difference in calibers, countries of origin, and the knowledge of the priority of the skills needed for development.

I hope you find this work useful and remember that a manual does not replace proper training and hands on experience. Please email comments to erik@vig-sec.com, particularly if you find any errors or glaring omissions.

Erik Lawrence

Table of Contents

M203

Grenade Launcher

Section 1

Introduction

The objective of this manual is to allow the reader to be able to use the various M203 40mm grenade launching weapons competently. The manual will give the reader background/specifications of the weapon, instructions on its operation, disassembly and assembly; proper firing procedure; and malfunction/misfire procedures. Operator-level maintenance will also be detailed to allow the reader to understand and become competent in the use and maintenance of the M203 Grenade Launcher.

Description

The M203 40mm Grenade Launcher is used while attached to an M4/M16A2 5.56mm rifle. It is a lightweight, compact, breech-loading, pump-action, single-shot launcher. The launcher consists of a hand guard and sight assembly with an adjustable metallic folding, short-range blade sight assembly, and an aluminum receiver assembly which houses the barrel latch, barrel stop, and firing mechanism. The launcher is capable of firing a variety of low-velocity 40mm ammunition. The launcher also has a quadrant sight, which may be attached to the M16A2 carrying handle and is used when precision is required out to the maximum effective range of the weapon. The M203 was designed and procured as the replacement for the M79 grenade launcher of the Vietnam era.

The M203 generally refers to the United States Army designation for a single-shot 40mm grenade launcher that attaches to the M16 assault rifle or the M4 Carbine. Stand-alone variants exist, as do versions capable of being used on many other rifles. The device attaches under the barrel and forward of the magazine, the trigger being just forward of the rifle magazine. The rifle magazine functions as a hand grip when firing the M203. A separate sighting system is added to rifles fitted with the M203, as the rifle's standard sights are not matched to the launcher. It creates a versatile combination weapon system capable of firing both 5.56mm rifle ammunition as well as the complete range of 40mm high-explosive and special purpose ammunition. The M203 can fire high-explosive, smoke, illuminating, buckshot direct fire, CS gas, and training grenades.

The characteristics of the M203/M203A1 Grenade Launcher:

1. COUNTRY OF ORIGIN: USA
2. MILITARY DESIGNATION: M203, M201A1, M203A2, M203 PI
3. CARTRIDGE TYPE: 40 x 46mm low power grenade cartridges
4. TYPE OF FEED: Single shot
5. LENGTH: Barrel- 9 inches/23 cm and 12 inches/30.5 cm
6. MUZZLE VELOCITY: 250 fps/76 mps

7. **WEIGHT**:
    a. **Launcher**: 3 pounds/1.4 kg
    b. **Rifle (M16A2)**: 8.8 pounds/ 4 kg
    c. **Total (including 30 rounds)**: 11.8 pounds/ 5.4 kg

8. **MAXIMUM EFFECTIVE RANGE**:
    a. **Area target**: 1150 feet/ 350 m
    b. **Point target**: 490 feet/150 m
    c. **Maximum range**: 1310 feet/ 400 m
    d. Minimum arming range: 45-125 feet/ 14-38 meters

9. **MINIMUM SAFE RANGE**:
    a. **Training**: 425 feet/ 130 m
    b. **Combat**: 100 feet/ 31 m

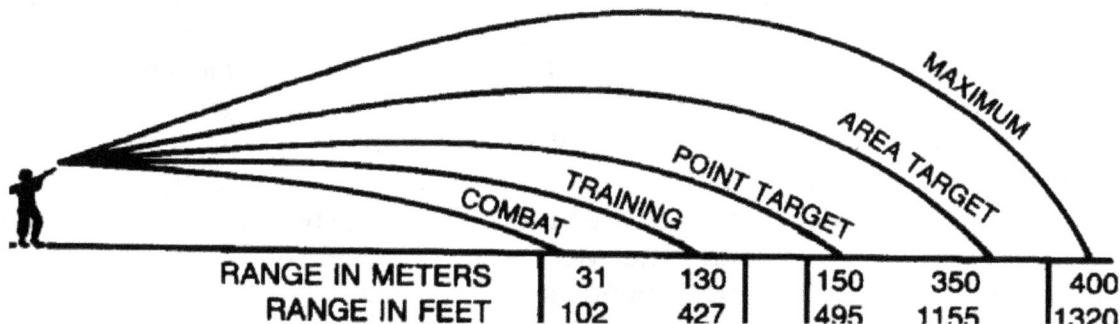

| RANGE IN METERS | 31 | 130 | 150 | 350 | 400 |
| RANGE IN FEET | 102 | 427 | 495 | 1155 | 1320 |

Figure 1-1 M203 Range Diagram

Background

The M203 was introduced to U.S. military forces during the early 1970s and replaced the older M79 grenade launcher and conceptually similar Colt XM148 design. However, while the M79 was a separate weapon entirely, the M203 was designed as a rifle attachment in order to increase the efficiency at which an operator could alternate between bullet fire and HE grenade fire.

A new grenade launcher in development, the XM320, will likely replace the 203 in United States service eventually. The XM320 weighs more than the M203, but has some added benefits.

The M203 40mm Grenade Launcher was designed and procured as the replacement for the M79 grenade launcher of the Vietnam era. In August 1969, the Army accepted the M203 40mm grenade launcher attachment for the M16A1 rifle. The M203 replaced the M79, uses the same ammunition, and provides the operator with a weapon that is both a rifle and a grenade launcher. The M79 served only as a launcher and deprived the rifle squad of two rifles. When Picatinny teamed the M203 Grenade Launcher with the M16A2 rifle, it gave a single infantryman more firepower than an entire infantry platoon with artillery support had in the Civil War.

Design

The M203 is a single-shot, breech-loading weapon with rifled barrel. The loading is achieved by sliding the aluminum barrel forward and then inserting the round of ammunition into the breech and sliding the loaded barrel back into the battery. The barrel is held in-battery by the manually controlled lock, which is disengaged by depressing the barrel catch lever at the left side of the launcher, above the middle of the barrel. The loaded cartridge is held at the breech face by the extractor claw and remains stationary when the barrel is opened forward. Once the barrel clears the fired case or unfired round, it is free to fall down from the breech face so the next round can be loaded if necessary. The self-cocking firing unit with its own trigger is located at the rear of the M203 receiver, also made from aluminum alloy. The manual safety in the form of the swinging flap is located inside the trigger guard, just ahead of the trigger. The rear part of the barrel is covered with a polymer handgrip. The standard M203 easily installs on the M16A1 and M16A2 rifle. If necessary, the M203 can be mounted on separate shoulder-stock/pistol-grip assemblies (available from several companies, such as Colt or Knight's Armament) to be used as a stand-alone weapon.

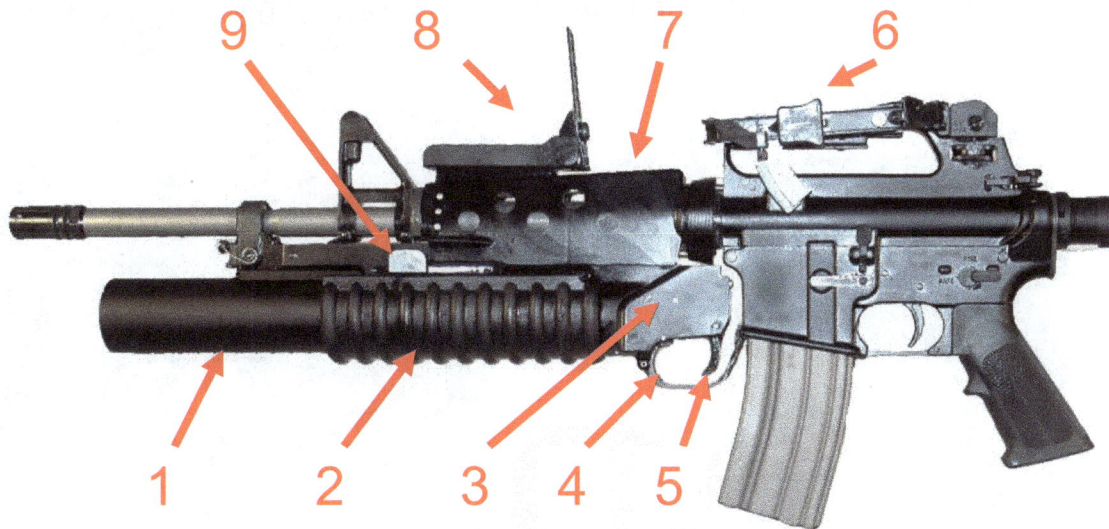

Figure1-2 Left side photo of launcher

M203 Grenade Launcher Nomenclature

1- Barrel	4- Safety (in FIRE position)	7- Handguard
2- Barrel Grip	5- Trigger	8- Leaf Sight
3- Receiver	6- Quadrant Sight	9- Barrel Latch

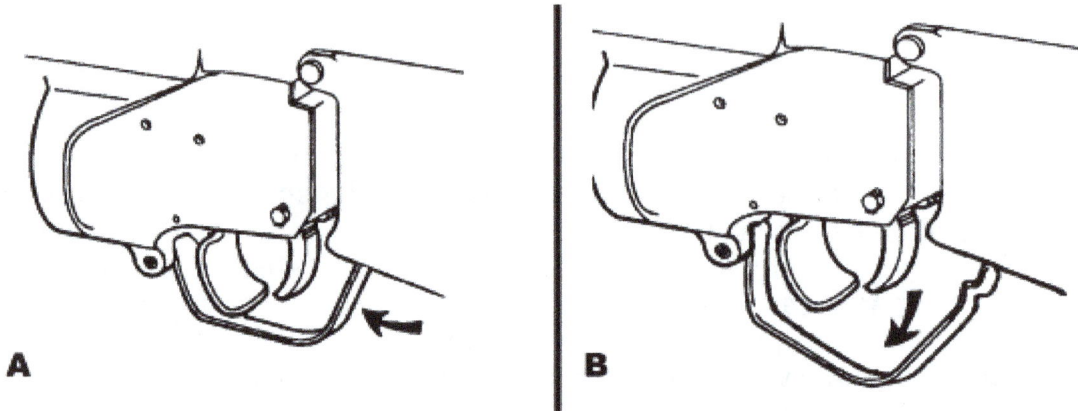

Figure 1-3a Trigger Guard | **1-3b Trigger Guard open for mittens**

Trigger Guard- The trigger guard protects the trigger. A complete self-cocking firing mechanism, including barrel latch, trigger, and positive safety lever, is included in the receiver, allowing the M203 to be operated as a completely independent weapon, even though attached to the M4 Carbine or the M16A2/A4 Rifle. Depressing the rear portion of the trigger guard rotates it down and away from the magazine well of the rifle, which allows the weapon to be fired while the firer is wearing gloves or mittens. LMT models are pinned and this pin must be removed to rotate the trigger guard for use with mittens. (Figures 1-3a & 1-3b).

Figure 1-4a Safety in FIRE position | **1-4b Safety in SAFE position**

Safety- The safety is inside the trigger guard, just in front of the trigger. For the launcher to fire, the safety must be forward. When the safety is rearward, the launcher is on SAFE. The safety is manually adjusted (Figures 1-4a & 1-4b).

Figure 1-5a M203 Receiver

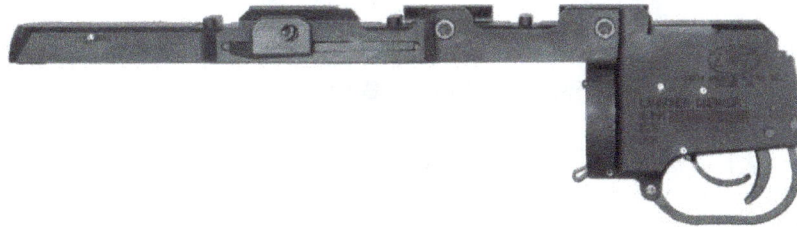

Figure 1-5b M203 LMT Rail Mount Receiver

Receiver Assembly and Serial Number- The receiver assembly houses the firing mechanism and ejection system and supports the barrel assembly. The receiver of the M203 is made of high-strength, forged aluminum alloy, which offers it extreme ruggedness, yet keeps weight to a minimum. On the left side of the receiver assembly is the launcher's serial number (Figures 1-5a and 1-5b).

Figure 1-6a M203 Barrel Assembly, 12 inch

Figure 1-6b M203 Barrel Assembly, 9 inch

Barrel Assembly- The barrel assembly holds the cartridges ready for firing and directs the projectile. The barrel, which is also made of a high-strength aluminum alloy, slides forward in the receiver to accept a round of ammunition and slides rearward to lock automatically in the closed position, ready to fire (Figures 1-6a and 1-6b).

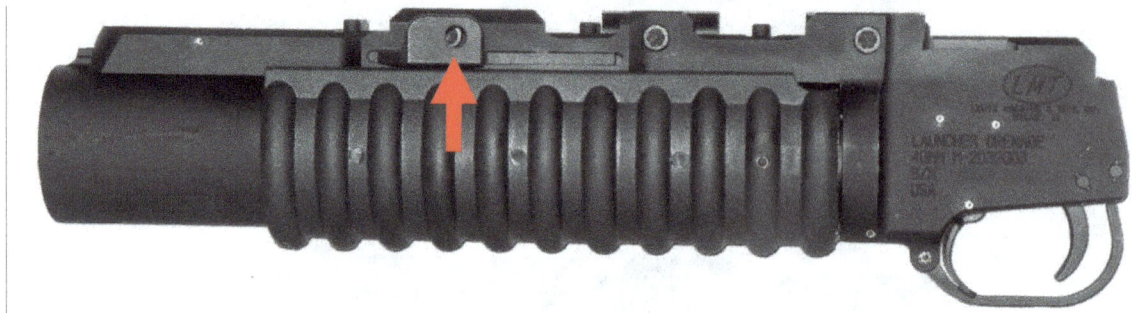

Figure 1-7 M203 Barrel Latch

Barrel Latch- On the left side of the barrel is a latch that locks the barrel and receiver together. To open the barrel, depress the barrel latch and slide the barrel forward (Figure 1-7).

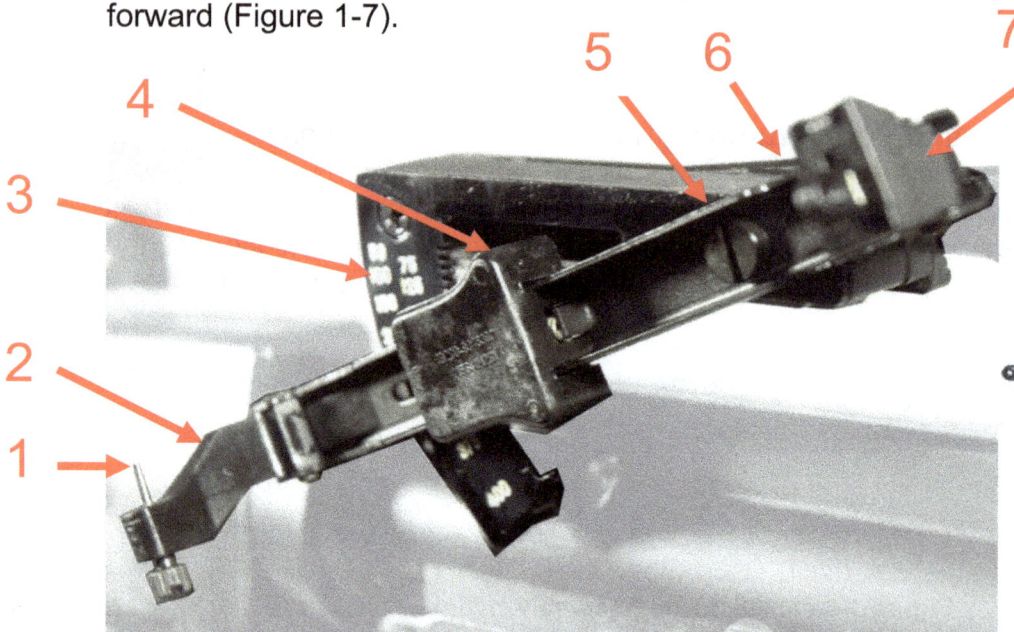

Figure1-8a Quadrant sight

Figure 1-8b On Rifle

Quadrant Sight Nomenclature

1- Front Sight
2- Front Sight Post Arm
3- Range Quadrant

4- Range Adjustment Latch
5- Mounting Screw
6- Rear Sight Aperture

7- Rear Sight Arm

Quadrant Sight Assembly- The quadrant sight assembly, which attaches to the left side of the rifle's carrying handle, enables the operator to adjust for elevation and windage. This assembly consists of the sight, mounting screw, sight latch, rear sight aperture, sight aperture arm, front sight post, and sight post arm (Figures 1-8a and 1-8b).

Clamp, Bracket Assembly, and Mounting Screw- The clamp and the bracket assembly hold the quadrant sight on the rifle's carrying handle. The mounting screw inserts through the right side of the clamp and into the bracket assembly.

1. **Sight Arm and Range Quadrant-** The sight arm mounts both the sight aperture arm (which holds the rear sight aperture) and the sight post arm (which holds the front sight post). This procedure allows the sight to pivot on the range quadrant to the desired range setting. The range quadrant is graduated in 25-meter increments from 50 to 400 meters. Applying rearward pressure on the sight latch releases the quadrant sight arm so it can move along the range quadrant. Centering the number in the rear sight aperture selects the desired range. Releasing the sight latch locks the sight in position (Figures 1-8a & 1-8b).

Figure1-8c Quadrant sight alignment

2. **Front Sight Post-** The front sight post mounts on the sight post arm by means of a pivot bracket. To prevent damage to the sights, keep the bracket closed when the sights are not in use. Use the sight post as follows to make minor adjustments in elevation when zeroing the launcher (Figure 1-8c):
   - To decrease elevation, turn the elevation adjustment screw on the sight post clockwise; to increase elevation, turn it counterclockwise.
   - To move the impact of the projectile 5 meters at a range of 200 meters, turn the elevation adjustment screw one full turn -- 360 degrees. To move the impact of the projectile 2.5 meters at a range of 200 meters, turn the elevation adjustment screw one half turn --180 degrees.

3. **Rear Sight Aperture-** The rear sight aperture is on the sight aperture arm, which is attached to the rear portion of the quadrant sight arm. Use the rear sight aperture as follows to make minor adjustments in deflection (windage) when zeroing the launcher:
   - To move the impact to the left, press the rear sight aperture retainer down and move the rear sight aperture away from the barrel; to move the impact to the right, move it toward the barrel.
   - To move the impact of the projectile 1.5 meters at a range of 200 meters, move the rear sight aperture one notch.

Figure1-9 Leaf sight, example of 200 Meter shot

Leaf Sight Nomenclature

1- Elevation Adjustment Screw
3- Windage Adjustment Screw

2- Elevation Adjustment Increments (10 m)
4- Windage Adjustment Increments (1.5 m)

Leaf Sight Assembly- The leaf sight assembly is attached to the top of the handguard. The leaf sight assembly consists of the sight, its base and mount, an elevation adjustment screw, and a windage adjustment screw. Elevation and windage scales are marked on the mount. The folding, adjustable, open-ladder design of the sight permits rapid firing without sight manipulation. The front sight post of the M16-series rifle serves as the front aiming post for the M203 leaf sight (Figure 1-9).

1. **Sight Base-** Two mounting screws permanently attach the sight base to the rifle handguard. When the sight is down or not in use, the base protects it from damage.

2. **Sight Mount and Sight-** The operator uses the sight mount, which is attached to the sight base, to raise or lower the sight. Though the range is not marked on the sight in meters, the sight is graduated in 50-meter increments from 50 to 250 meters, which are marked with a "1" at 100 meters and a "2" at 200 meters.

3. **Elevation Adjustment Screw and Elevation Scale-** The screw attaches the sight to its mount. When the screw is loosened, the sight can be moved

up or down to make minor adjustments in elevation during the zeroing procedure. The rim of a 40mm cartridge case is useful for turning the screw. Raising the sight increases the range; lowering the sight decreases the range. The elevation scale consists of five lines spaced equally on the sight. The index line is to the left of the sight. Moving the sight one increment moves the impact of the projectile 10 meters in elevation at a range of 200 meters.

4. **Windage Screw and Windage Scale-** The knob on the left end of the windage screw is used to make minor deflection adjustments during the zeroing procedure. The scale has a zero line in its center and two lines spaced equally on each side of the zero line. At a range of 200 meters, turning the knob on the windage scale one increment to the left moves the impact of the projectile 1.5 meters to the right.

Knight's Armament M203 Reflex Quadrant Optical Sight

Figure 1-10a Reflex Quadrant Sight   1-10b Reflex Quadrant Sight on M203, right side

The sight is operated by first removing the reflex sight's protective cover (not pictured). The sight's red aiming dot automatically turns "ON" as the cover is removed. The user then sets the desired range on the range quadrant's elevation scale. This is accomplished by retracting the elevation latch back towards the reflex sight while moving the quadrant sight arm up or down until the desired range appears in the range window. *For right-handed operator only.* Left-handed unit is available via special order. Mounts directly to M203 receiver and works with (newer) Knight's (Figures 1-10a & 1-10b).

Lewis Machine and Tool (LMT) Rail Mounted Quadrant Sight

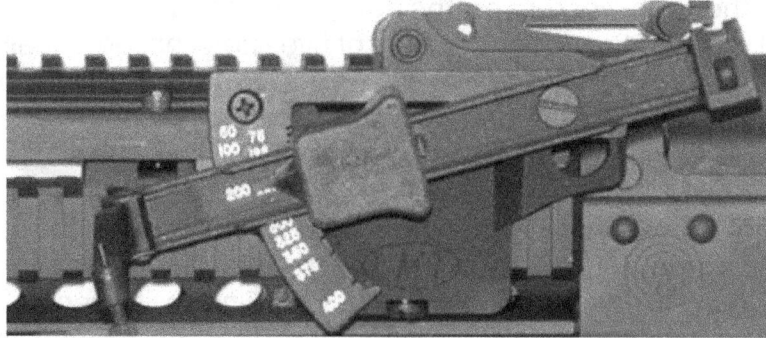

Figure 1-11 LMT Rail Mounted Quadrant Sight

Identical operation as the standard quadrant sight that attaches to the M16/M4 carrying handle but this sight is designed to be mounted on the left side of a Picatinny Rail forearm of an M4, M16A4 or AK-47/74 rifles.

LMT M203 Rail Mounted Launcher on AK type rifles

Figure 1-12 LMT Rail Mounted Launcher on AKM, close view

Figure 1-13 LMT Rail Mounted Launcher on AKM, full view

Operation

TECHNICAL PRINCIPLES OF OPERATION

1. Open the launcher barrel, insert a round, and close the launcher barrel.

2. Place launcher on safe.

3. Place the launcher to your shoulder. Keep muzzle pointed at target and move the safety from the safe to the fire position.

4. Align the front and rear sights with the target and squeeze the trigger.

5. Squeezing the trigger releases the firing pin and allows it to impact the primer on the round.

6. The primer ignites the propellant in the round.

7. Gas from the burning propellant pushes the projectile along the barrel of the launcher.

8. The rifling in the barrel causes the projectile to rotate, which provides stability during flight to the target.

CYCLE OF FUNCTIONING

It is essential to know the M203's cycle of functioning from loading to firing to help operators recognize and correct stoppages. Many of the actions described in this chapter occur at once, but here they are explained separately.

1. **Unlocking**. The cycle begins when the operator depresses the barrel latch to unlock the barrel assembly and slides the barrel assembly forward (Figure 1-14).

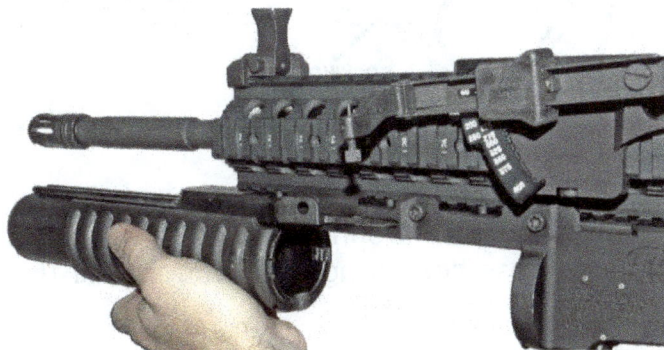

Figure 1-14 Unlocking the barrel assembly

2. **Cocking**. The operator moves the barrel assembly forward, then backward, to cock the weapon. As the barrel assembly moves, it takes with it the barrel extension. Their movement causes the following to occur:

   A. The cocking lever is forced down as the barrel assembly and barrel extension, which are interlocked with the cocking lever, move forward.

   B. The movement of the cocking lever forces the spring-loaded firing pin to the rear.

   C. The spring-loaded follower also moves forward with the barrel extension.

   D. The barrel assembly continues forward, disengaging the barrel extension from the cocking lever. The cocking lever is then held down by the follower.

   E. When the operator begins to move the barrel assembly back to the rear, this forces the follower to the rear.

   F. The cocking lever again engages the barrel extension, which causes the firing pin to move slightly forward and engage the primary trigger sear. This cocks the weapon (Figure 1-15).

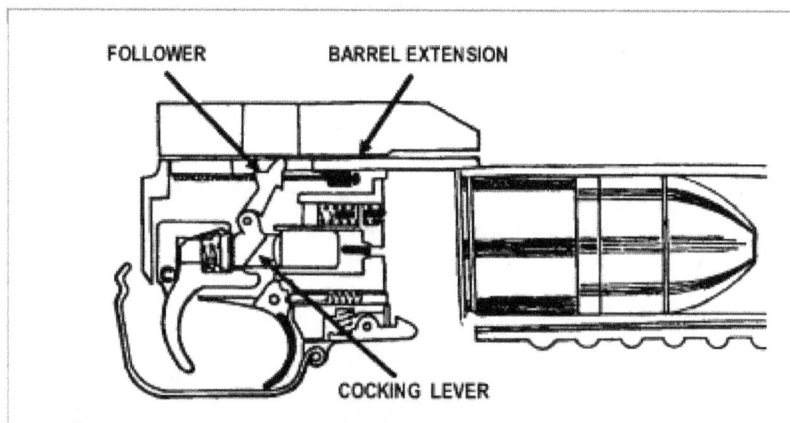

Figure 1-15 Cocking the M203 grenade launcher

3. **Extracting**. Extracting and cocking occur at the same time. As the operator opens the barrel assembly, a spring-loaded extractor keeps the live round or spent cartridge case seated against the receiver until the barrel clears the cartridge case (Figure 1-16).

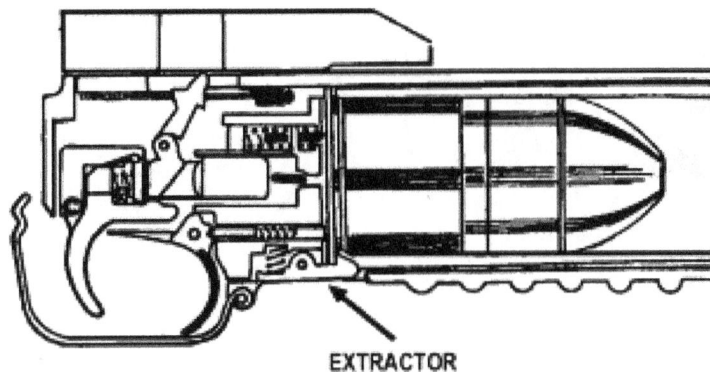

Figure 1-16 Extracting the round or cartridge case

4. **Ejecting**. The spring-loaded ejector pushes the live round or spent cartridge case from the barrel assembly (Figure 1-17).

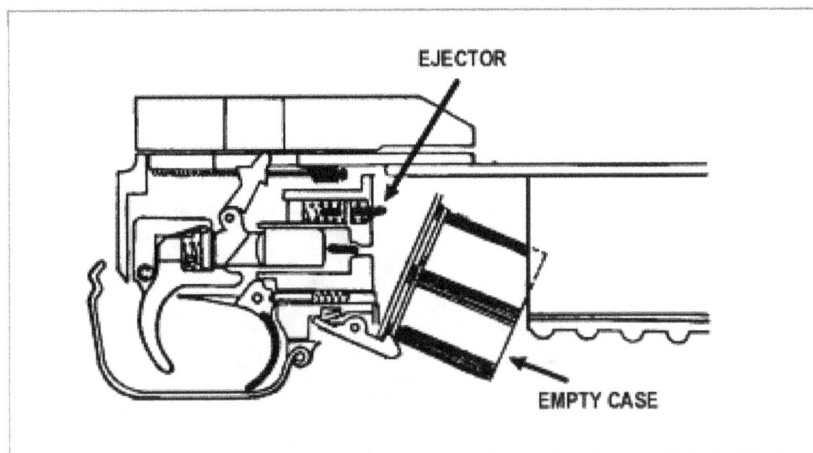

Figure 1-17 Ejecting the round or cartridge case

5. **Loading**. With the barrel assembly open, the operator inserts a round into the breech end of the barrel (Figures 1-18a, 1-18b & 1-18c).

Figure 1-18a Insert round   **Figure 1-18b Slide barrel back to receiver**

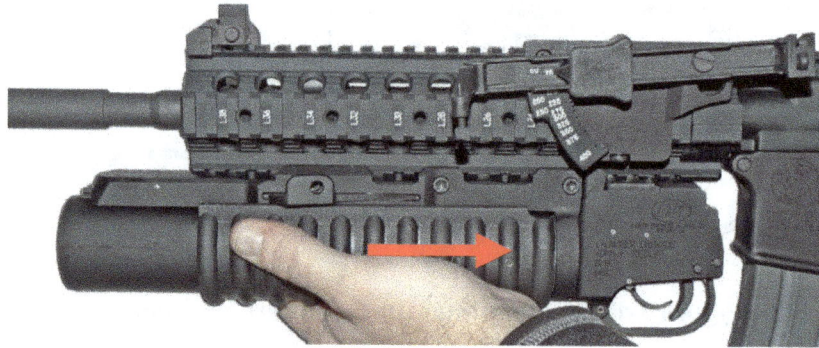

Figure 1-18c Locking the M203 grenade launcher, listening for the CLICK

6. **Chambering**. As the operator closes the breech end of the barrel assembly, the extractor contacts the rim of the cartridge and seats (chambers) the round firmly (Figure 1-19).

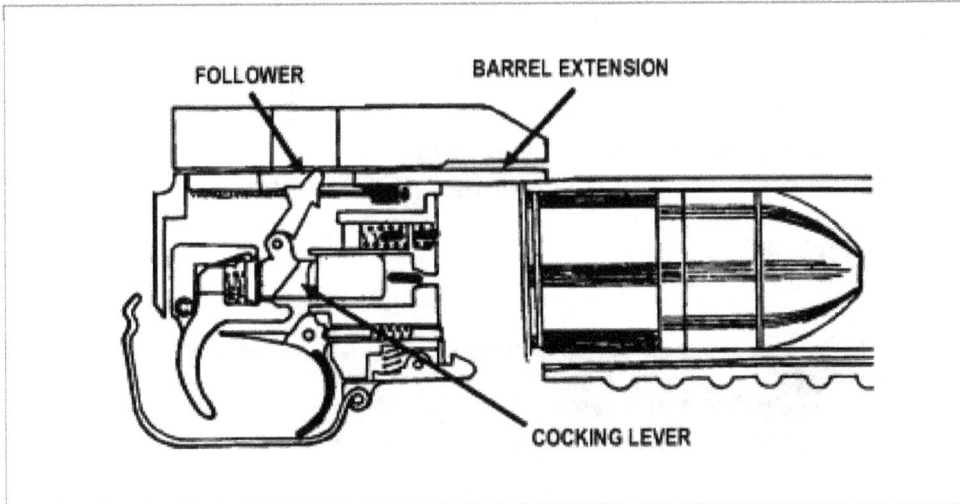

Figure 1-19 Chambering a round

7. **Locking**. As the barrel assembly closes, the barrel latch engages it. The cocking lever engages the barrel extension so that it cannot move forward along the receiver assembly.

8. **Firing**. When the operator pulls the trigger, the primary trigger sear disengages from the bottom sear surface of the firing pin. This releases the spring-driven firing pin, forcing it forward against the cartridge primer (Figure 1-20).

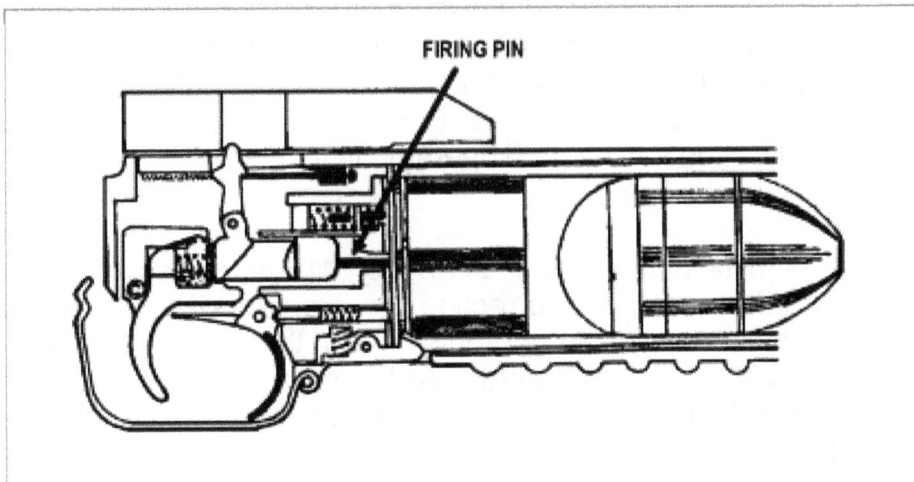

Figure 1-20 Firing the M203 grenade launcher

Variants

There are numerous variants of the M203 manufactured in the U.S., and throughout the world, for various applications. These vary chiefly in the length of the barrel, attachment type, and quick detach (QD) capability.

XM148/Colt CG-4

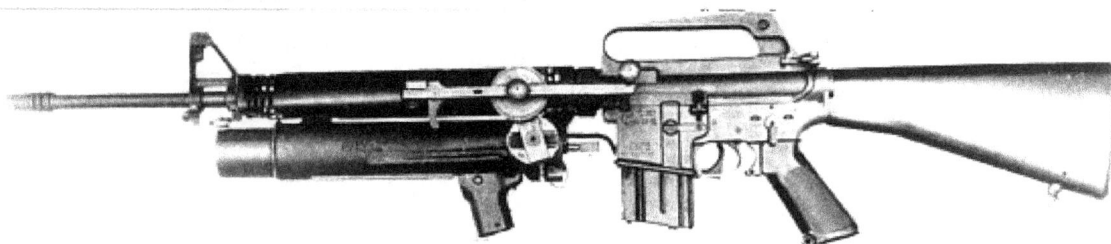

Figure 1-21 XM148/Colt CGL-4 Grenade Launcher

Caliber: 40mm
Type: Single Shot
Overall length: 16.5 inches/ 42 cm
Weight unloaded: 3 pounds/ 1.4 kilograms
Barrel length: 10 inches/ 25 cm

The XM148 served as a proof of concept for a more successful M203 grenade launcher. It was an experimental 40mm grenade launcher developed by Colt Firearms as the CGL-4 (Colt Grenade Launcher). Colt manufactured the launcher for field testing during the Vietnam era. Early grenades armed upon firing and made a dangerous situation for the operator if the round bounced back from branches or excessive foliage.

It was designed for installation below the barrel of M16-type rifles and was intended to replace the stand-alone M79, correcting the problem of operators relying on pistols as a secondary weapon. After problems with the experimental design were discovered, the XM148 was replaced by AAI Corporation's conceptually similar M203 design, currently the primary grenade launcher used by the U.S. armed forces and others today.

The launcher's barrel could slide forward to accept a single 40mm round into the breech. It came with a primitive version of the quadrant sight later used with the M203. It differed from the later model by featuring an external cocking handle and an extended trigger that allowed the weapon to be fired without removing the hand from the rifle's pistol grip. This same extended trigger was also one source of the weapon's problems as it allowed accidental discharges of a loaded weapon if caught by tree branches, gear, or anything else capable of overcoming the 6- to 11-pound trigger pull.

M203 Grenade Launcher

Figure 1-22 M203 Grenade Launcher

NSN: 1010-00-179-6447
Caliber: 40mm
Type: Single Shot
Overall length: 15 inches/ 38 cm
Weight unloaded: 3 pounds/ 1.4 kilograms
Weight loaded: 3.6 pounds/ 1.6 kilograms
Weight with M16A2: 11 pounds/ 5 kilograms
Barrel length: 12 inches/ 30 cm
Height (below rifle barrel): 3.3 inches/ 8 cm
Width: 3.3 inches/ 8 cm

The standard M203 is intended for permanent (armorer level) attachment to the M16A1, M16A2, and M16A3 rifles and utilizes a 12" rifled barrel. Each M203 is furnished with a special handguard. A battle sight adjustable for ranges of 50 to 250 meters is mounted on the handguard. A quadrant sight, which mounts on the carrying handle and is adjustable for 50 to 400 meters, is also furnished with each launcher. These can also be attached to M4 and M4A1 carbines using a different front attachment point forward of the front sight block, but the M4 SOPMOD kit uses M203A1 grenade launchers.

M203A1 Grenade Launcher

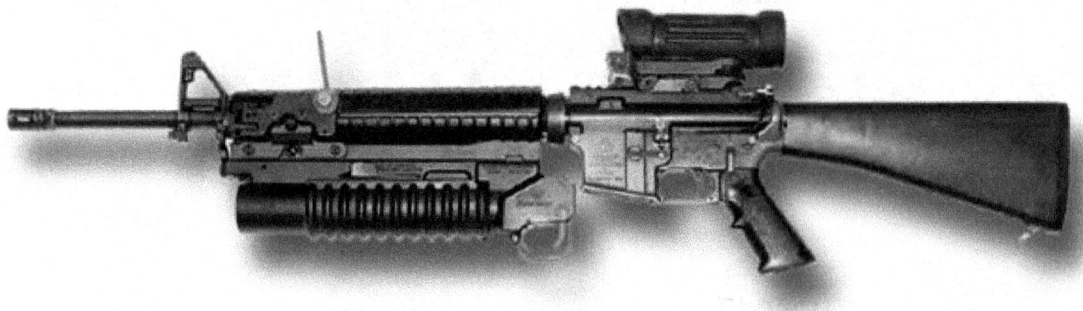

Figure 1-23 M203A1 Grenade Launcher on Diemaco M16A4

NSN: 1010-01-410-7422
Caliber: 40mm
Type: Single Shot
Overall length: 12 inches/ 30 cm
Barrel length: 9 inches/ 23 cm

The American M203A1 is intended for use with the M4 and M4A1 carbine. The M203A1 has a short barrel for airborne applications and a quick-release mechanism to allow the user to tailor the weapon to individual missions. The barrel is shortened to 9", and principally the M203A1 QD is able to detach quickly from the rifle and be replaced by a Knight's Armament Company M4 RAS lower handguard. An advantage of using a 40mm grenade launcher on an assault rifle equipped with MIL-STD 1913 rails is the attachment of various range-finding optics.

The Canadian M203A1 by Diemaco (now Colt Canada) was a similar design with a different mounting system that did not require mounting points of the same profile as the M16A1 rifles. The weapon's 9" barrel slides forward further than the standard American models to allow longer rounds to be loaded. This model is identifiable by the increased distance between the grenade launcher's barrel axis and the rifle's. This weapon may no longer be in production.

M203A2 Grenade Launcher

Figure 1-24 M16A4 with M203A2 Grenade Launcher

Caliber: 40mm
Type: Single Shot
Overall length: 15 inches/ 38 cm
Weight unloaded: 3 pounds/ 1.4 kilograms
Weight loaded: 3.6 pounds/ 1.6 kilograms
Weight with M16A2: 11 pounds/ 5 kilograms
Barrel length: 12 inches/ 30 cm
Height (below rifle barrel): 3.3 inches/ 8 cm
Width: 3.3 inches/ 8 cm

The M203A2 is intended for use with the M16A4 MWS (Modular weapon system). Using standard 12" barrels, the grenade launcher is intended for use in concert with the Knight's Armament Company M5 RAS. Again, an advantage of this system is the attachment of range-finding optics that make precision targeting easier.

M203 P1 Grenade Launcher

Figure 1-25 M203 P1 Grenade Launcher

The **M203 PI** system is used for attachment of the M203 to other rifles, including but not limited to the Steyr AUG, H&K G3 and other rifles, and even the MP5 submachine gun. Most of these other companies have since devised 40mm grenade launchers custom integrated with the weapon. This model is a commercial product from R/M Equipment that uses interbars to fit a variety of firearms.

Lewis Machine & Tool (LMT) Rail Mounted M203 Grenade Launcher, 9- and 12-inch Models

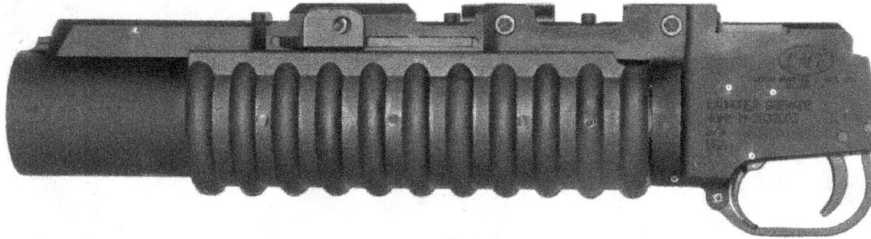

Figure 1-26 LMT 9" Rail Mounted M203 Grenade Launcher

Figure 1-27 LMT 12" Rail Mounted M203 Grenade Launcher

Proprietary launcher designed for use with the LMT Monolithic Rail Platform and other 1913 rail systems. LMT is an approved contractor for the M203, manufacturing them to government specifications. It is suitable to handle the recoil of the 40mm round, easy to install, and field removable, with a low-profile design. Twist rate on the launchers is 1:48".

M320 Grenade Launcher Module (GLM)

Figure 1-28a M320 Grenade Launcher Module (GLM)   **Figure 1-28b Breech opens left**

Caliber: 40mm
Type: Single Shot, Left-side load
Overall length: 14 inches/ 35 cm
Weight unloaded: 3.3 pounds/ 1.5 kilogram
Weight loaded: 3.7 pounds/ 1.7 kilograms
Barrel length: 11 inches/ 28 cm

The M320 Grenade Launcher Module (GLM), a derivative of the German-made AG-36, is a low-velocity grenade launcher manufactured by Heckler & Koch. The XM320 is a 40mm grenade-launching weapon module that will replace selected M203 series grenade launchers currently mounted on the M16/M4 series of rifles and carbines and will also provide a grenade-launching capability for the Objective Individual Combat Weapon Increment I system. The M320 40mm grenade launcher can be used in a standalone mode when the add-on, multi-position sliding buttstock is added, or as a separable under-barrel module with the M16 rifle, the M4 carbine, or the XM8 carbine.

The integral day/night sighting system provides accurate grenade fire out to the maximum effective range of fielded ammunition. The open-architecture attachment system enables mounting on M16A2, M16A4, M4, and OICW Increment I rifles and carbines. The unrestricted breech mechanism allows the use of longer ammunition than currently fielded, ensuring a degree of system growth. It is lighter, safer, and more reliable than the M203 through the use of lighter materials and a more modern trigger/firing system.

M203 Grenade Launcher on Stock Platform

Three position
collapsible stock
with rubber buttpad

Figure 1-29 Knight's Armament M203 GL Standalone Buttstock Module

Figure1-30 Knight's Armament M203 GL Standalone Buttstock Module, Folded

Made by Knight's Armament (Item number BH-96241) with a three-position collapsible stock and multiple sling attachment points. Includes rear leaf sight (100-350 meters), front fixed sight, and two quick-release push-button 1 1/4" sling swivels.

Other 40mm Grenade Launchers

Figre1-31 FN F2000 with a M203 GL type

Figre1-32 Steyr AUG 3 with a M203 GL type

CTS 40mm Tactical Launchers- With today's interest in target-specific munitions, the rifled 40mm system is rapidly gaining popularity. It is able to deploy all the recently developed direct-fire impact and barricade rounds, as well as all of the traditional crowd control and pyrotechnic gas rounds. CTS offer three 40mm launchers to meet the needs of today's military and law enforcement professional.

Various CTS Launchers:

Figre1-33 MODEL TGL-1 SINGLE SHOT (BH-CTS-TGL-1)

A rugged and reliable top-break design equipped with an ambidextrous barrel release mechanism. This system is compatible with all 40mm MIL SPEC rounds. The TGL-1 is a double-action-only launcher that incorporates a new iron sight, adjustable for windage and elevation, and will also accepts Picatinny ready optical sights.

The TGL-1 40mm launcher is designed to be compatible with all MIL SPEC less-lethal rounds. It is equipped with a trigger lock for safety and a barrel release latch that can be operated from both sides of the launcher. The TGL-1 can launch various grenades when fitted with an appropriate launching cup and using a launching cartridge. The TGL-1 is available with a composite fixed stock.

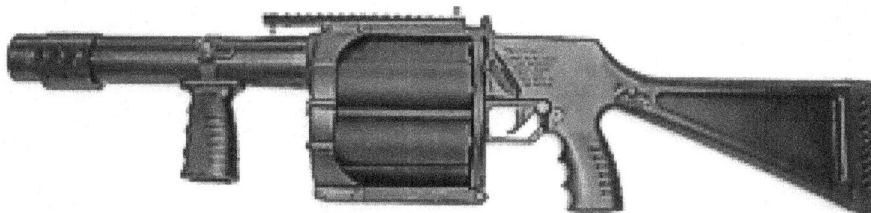

Figre1-34 MODEL TGL-6 MULTI-SHOT (BH-CTS-TGL-6)

The TGL-6 tactical launcher is a rotary spring-loaded 6-shot magazine system that can fire up to six 40mm rounds in rapid succession. The TGL-6 provides military and law enforcement users the security of having six rounds at their immediate disposal, reducing the risk of escalation between reloads. It can launch all MIL SPEC less-lethal rounds.

The TGL-6 is equipped with a trigger lock. Keeping the percussion primer on the cartridge and the firing pin out of line until a full trigger pull is performed provides additional safety. This mechanism virtually eliminates the risk of accidental discharge from rough handling. The TGL-6 is an excellent and cost-effective force multiplier.

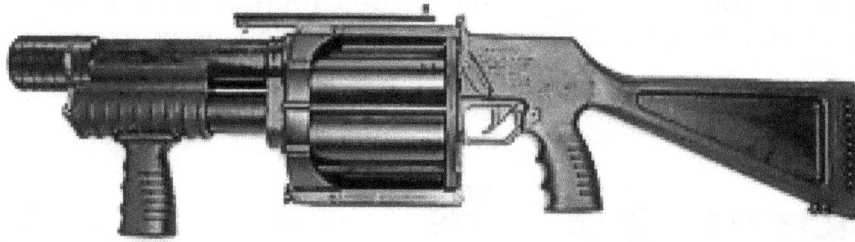

Figre1-35 MODEL PGL-65 40mm LAUNCHER (BH-PGL-65)

The PGL-65 is a pump-action 6-shot rotary system which eliminates the necessity of winding a spring-loaded magazine.

Physical Specifications

	TGL-1	TGL-6	PGL-65
Operating System	Single-Shot Action	Spring Motor-driven Magazine	Pump-action Magazine
Safety	Trigger Lock	Trigger Lock. Out of Line Mechanism	Trigger Lock. Out of Line Mechanism
Caliber	40mm	40mm	37/38 mm
Weight	2.24 kg (6.0 lb)	3.7 kg (9.9 lb)	4.85 kg (11 lb)
Total Length	749.3mm (29.5")	838.2 mm (33")	863.6 mm (34")
Barrel	355.6mm (14") Rifled Bore	228.6 mm (9") Smooth Bore	304.8 mm (12") Smooth Bore
Ejection	Extractor Assisted	Gravity	Gravity

Section 2

Maintenance

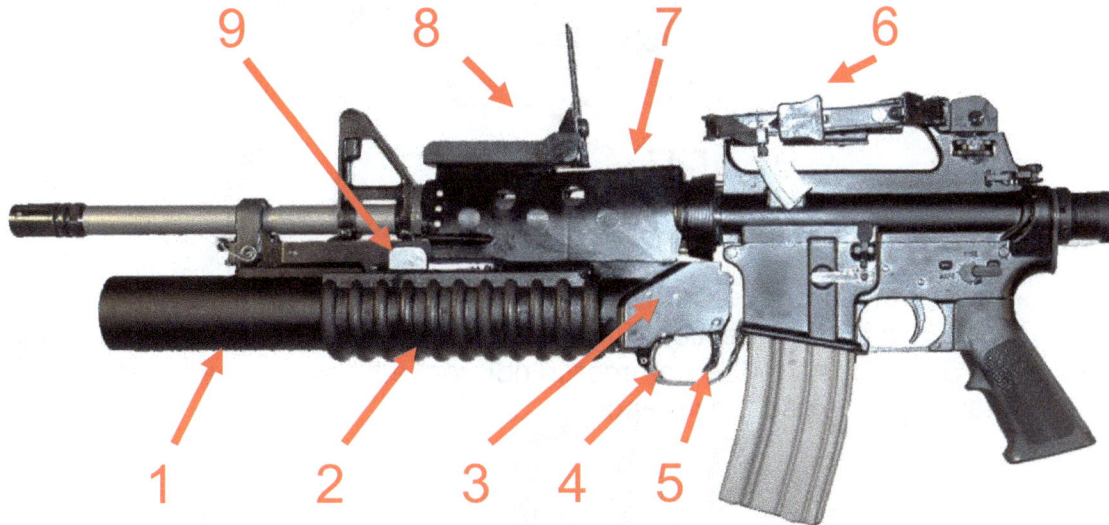

Figure 2-1 Photo of the M203 Grenade Launcher

1- Barrel	4- Safety (in FIRE position)	7- Handguard
2- Barrel Grip	5- Trigger	8- Leaf Sight
3- Receiver	6- Quadrant Sight	9- Barrel Latch

Clearing the M203

The operator must clear the rifle/carbine/grenade launcher before performing maintenance on it. Refer to the AR/15/M16/M4 manual, which provides instructions for clearing an M16-series rifle.

To clear the grenade launcher and orient it in a safe direction,

SAFE

Figure 2-2 M203 Safety

1. Ensure the grenade launcher is on safe (safety rearward position) and pointed in a safe direction (Figure 2-2). If the safety cannot be positioned in the SAFE position the hammer is not cocked, open the action to cock and allow you to place the weapon on SAFE.

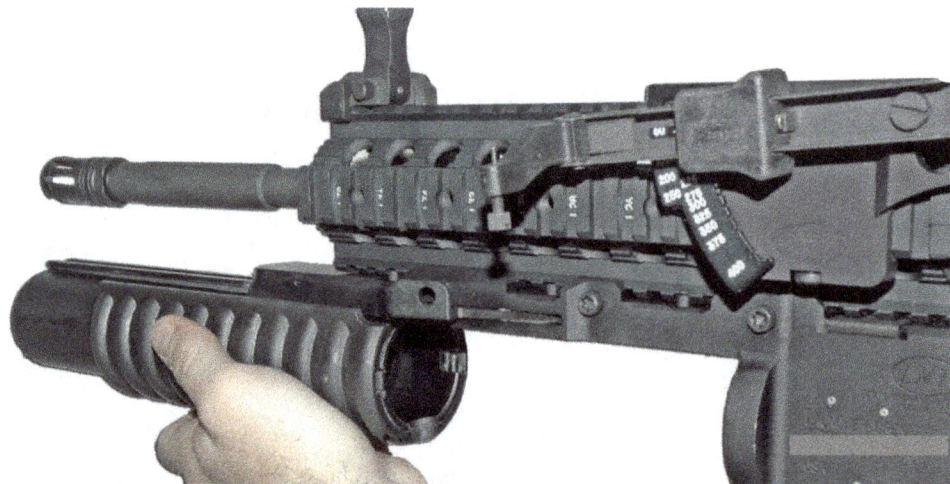

Figure 2-3

2. Push in the barrel latch and push the barrel forward, observe the round extracting, if present, and retain the round-do not let it drop (Figure 2-3).

Figure 2-4 Note- round in chamber

3. Visually and physically check the chamber for a round (Figure 2-4). Once you have ensured the grenade launcher has no round in it, you now can close the action. Pull the barrel to the rear until it clicks.

Figure 2-5a FIRE Position

Figure 2-5b SAFE position

4. Place the grenade launcher on FIRE (safety forward position); for disassemble or maintenance or on SAFE (safety rearward position) for carrying/storage. (Figures 2-5a and 2-5b)

Disassembling the M203 Grenade Launcher

NOTE- Place the grenade launcher's parts on a flat, clean surface with the muzzle oriented in a safe direction. This step aids in reassembly and simplifies the task of keeping up with the parts. (Only armorer-qualified personnel disassemble the grenade launcher beyond the steps described here.)

When the operator begins to disassemble the grenade launcher, it should be done in the following order:

M203 Model on an M16A2 type rifle

    A. Clear the Grenade Launcher and leave the barrel forward in the open position with the safety off.

    B. Loosen the mounting screw and remove the quadrant sight assembly from the carrying handle of the M16-series rifle carrying handle, (Figure 2-6).

Figure 2-6 Mounting Screw to loosen

    C. To remove the M203 barrel assembly.

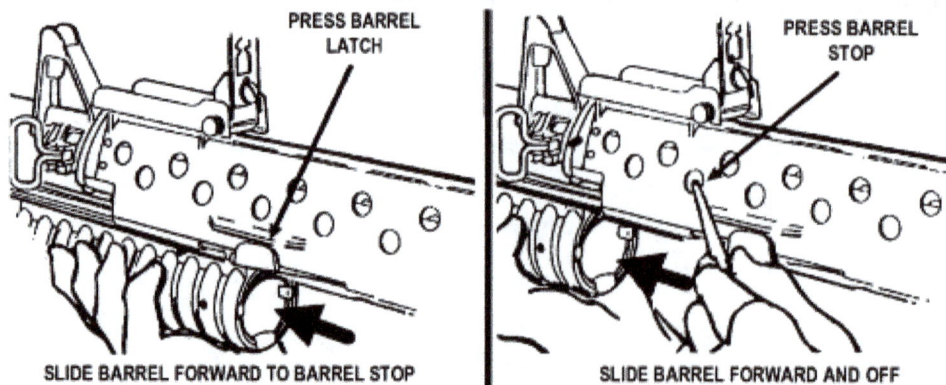

Figure 2-7a Slide barrel forward

Figure 2-7b Depress barrel stop

1. Push the barrel latch and move the barrel forward until it hits the barrel stop (Figure 2-7a).

2. On the left side of the handguard, insert a cleaning rod into the fourth hole back from the muzzle, depress the barrel stop, and slide the barrel forward and off, (Figure 2-7b).

3. Rest the trigger guard against the frame.

D. To remove the handguard assembly of non-Picatinny rail-mounted models.

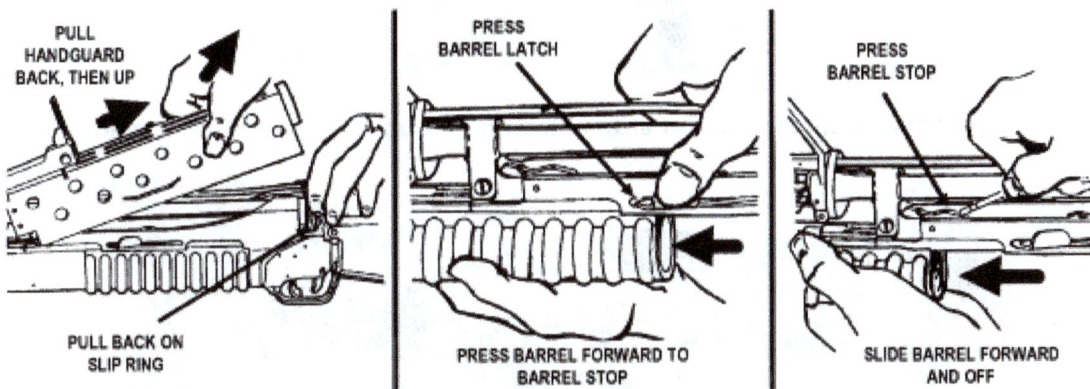

Figure 2-8

Pull back on the M16's slip ring and remove the handguard by pulling it up and back (Figure 2-8).

LMT M203 Rail Mounted Model on an M4 or AK type rifle

A. Clear the Grenade Launcher and leave the barrel forward in the open position with the safety off.

B. Loosen the mounting screw (use a flat tip screwdriver) and remove the quadrant sight assembly from the Picatinny rail, (Figure 2-9).

Figure 2-9 Mounting Screw to loosen

C. To remove the M203 barrel assembly,

1. Push the barrel latch and move the barrel forward until it hits the barrel stop.

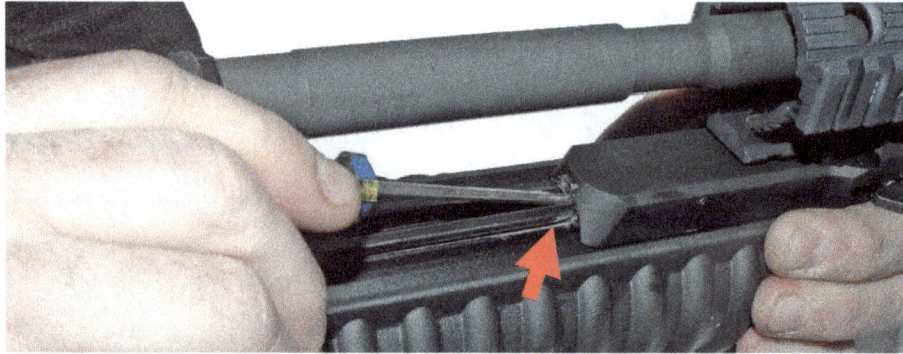

Figure 2-10a Locate the barrel stop catch and lift up (there is spring tension)

Figure 2-10b Maintain upward pressure on the barrel stop catch and slide barrel assembly forward

Figure 2-10c Slide barrel assembly forward until free of receiver rail

2. On the top of the barrel assembly, insert a flat tip screwdriver onto the top of the barrel stop catch, lift up the barrel stop catch, and slide the barrel forward and off. (Figure 2-10a-c)

D. To remove the M203 receiver from Picatinny rails.

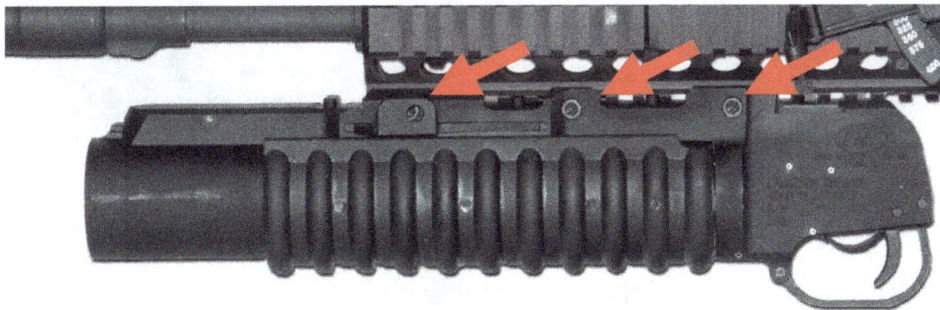

Figure 2-11

With a 5/32" or Torx T-25 hex key loosen the three hex screws and remove the receiver from the lower rail. If the receiver is not to be put back on the rail, hand-tighten the hex screws so they are not lost in storage. (Figure 2-11)

Cleaning and Lubrication

1. **Bore**. Attach a clean, dry rag to the thong and thoroughly moisten the rag with Cleaner, Lubricant, and Protectant (CLP). Pull the rag through the bore several times. Attach the bore brush to the thong, pull it through the bore several times, and follow this step with more rags moistened with CLP. Pull dry rags through the bore, and inspect each rag as it is removed. The bore is clean when a dry rag comes out clean. Finally, pull a rag lightly moistened with CLP through the bore to leave a light coat of lubricant inside the barrel. The best option to clean the bore is a BH-34040 40mm Boresnake pull-through cleaner, which has a built on brass brush and swab. Apply a healthy amount of CLP type solvent to the brass brush and the swab in front of the wire brush to break up the fouling and pull the swab through for one-pass cleaning.

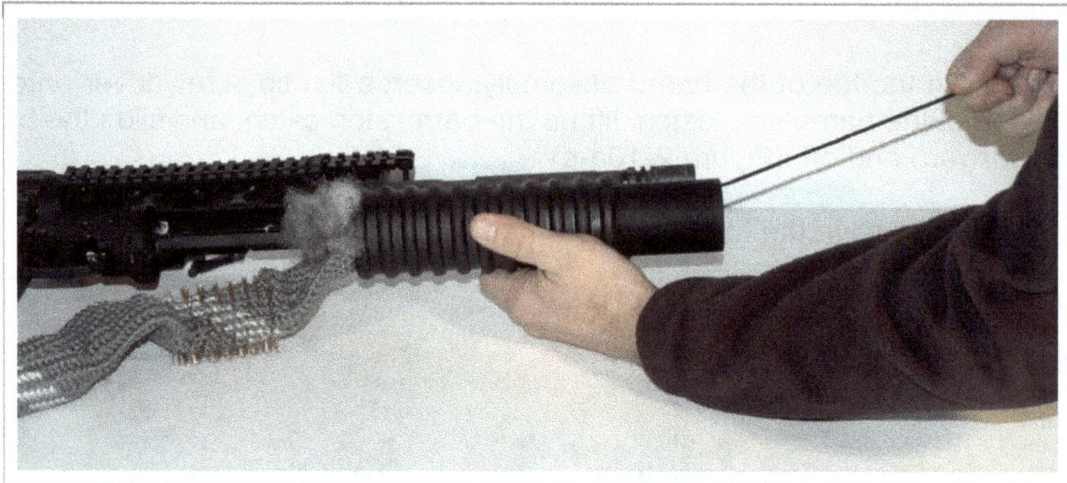

Figure 2-12 Cleaning the barrel with a 40mm Boresnake (BH-34040)

2. **Breech Insert**. Clean the face of the breech insert with a patch and CLP. Remove this CLP with dry rags; then lubricate the breech with a new, light coat of CLP.

3. **Other Parts**. Use a brush and dry rags to clean all the other parts and surfaces. After cleaning, apply a light coat of CLP to the outside of the launcher.

4. **Safety Mechanism**. Clean the safety mechanism properly with CLP; then lubricate it with CLP. (Figures 2-13).

LUBRICATION (CONT)

3 With barrel installed, apply a few drops of CLP (item 1, app D) through firing pin hole. Keep weapon pointed up 10-15 seconds. Cycle weapon and squeeze trigger to spread the oil.

4 Turn launcher upside down and lubricate safety detent with CLP (item 1, app D). It's in the receiver in front of the safety.

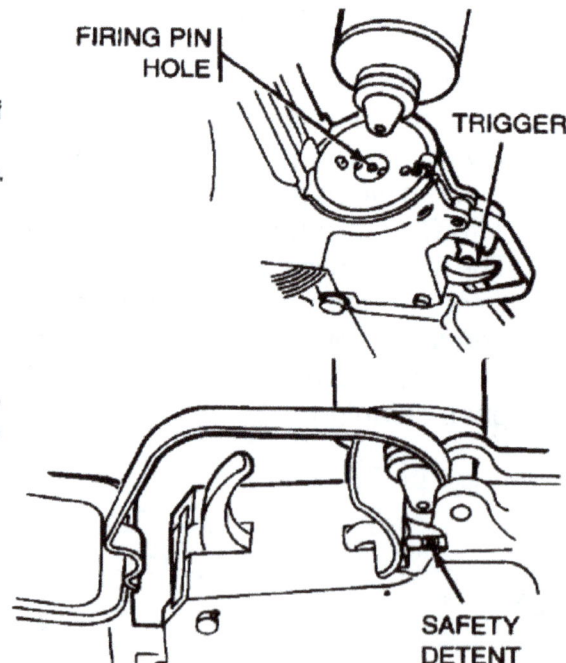

Figure 2-13 Lubricating the safety mechanism and firing pin hole

5. **Special Lubrication Requirements**. Keep the weapon clean and lubed with CLP. Lubricate the grenade launcher only with CLP and IAW the following environmental guidelines:
   A. **Extreme Heat**. Lubricate with CLP, grade 2.

   B. **Damp or Salty Air**. Clean the weapon and apply CLP, grade 2, frequently. Rainy, humid, and salty air contaminate the lube and cause corrosion. Inspect grenade launcher daily. Dry, clean, and lubricate as necessary.

   C. **Sandy or Dusty Air**. Clean the weapon and apply CLP, grade 2, frequently. Remove excess CLP with a rag after each application. Clean often. Oil frequently because heat dissolves the oil rapidly. Wipe oil from exposed surfaces. Cover weapon as much as possible. Keep sand out of parts.

   D. **Temperatures Below Freezing**. When the weapon is brought in from a cold area to a warm area, keep it wrapped in a parka or blanket, and allow it to reach room temperature gradually. If condensation forms on the weapon, dry and lubricate it at room temperature with CLP, grade 2, before returning it to cold weather. Otherwise, ice will form inside the mechanism.

   E. **After immersion in water,** disassemble, clean, oil, and reassemble as soon as possible. Make sure launcher is dry.

Inspecting the M203 Grenade Launcher

1. Inspection begins with the weapon already disassembled into its major groups or assemblies. Parts with shiny surfaces are serviceable.

   A. **All Parts**. Check for wear, corrosion, moisture, foreign matter, and damage, including burrs, scratches, dents, and nicks.

   B. **Handguard**. Check for cracks, dents, or distortion that prevents its firm attachment to the rifle.

   C. **Leaf Sight Assembly**. Check for bent or damaged parts, rust or corrosion, and illegibility of markings.

   D. **Barrel**. Check for cracks or dents.

   E. **Cartridge and Retainers**. Check for breakage, bends, chips, or missing parts.

BREECH
INSERT

Check for loose or pro-
truding breech insert.

FIRE

SAFE

Check safe and fire posi-
tions

BARREL
STOP

LATCH

Check barrel stop
and latch.

Figure 2-14 Points to inspect

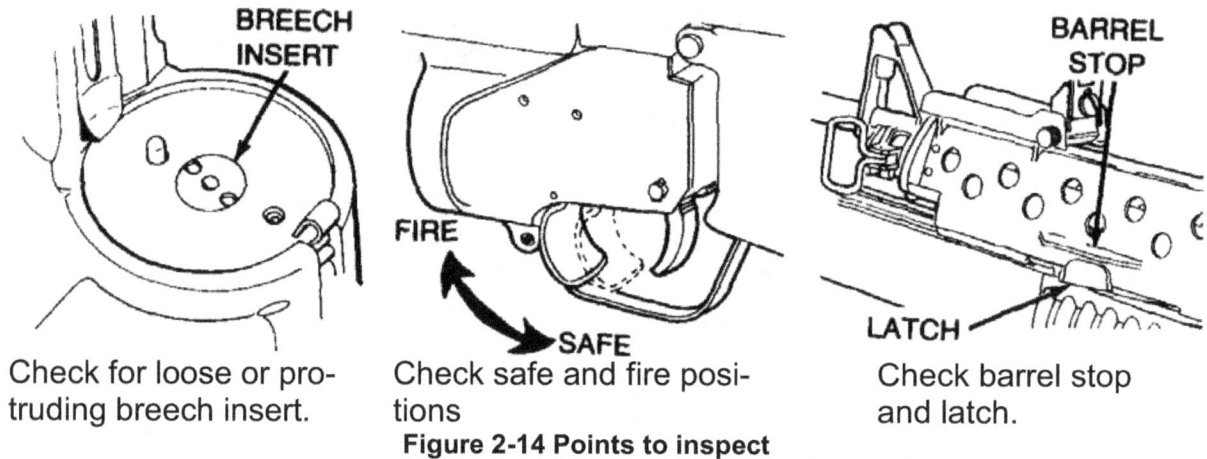

Reassembling the M203 Grenade Launcher

The operator will assemble the grenade launcher in the reverse order that he disassembled it.

1. Install the barrel by pressing the barrel stop and sliding the barrel into the receiver (Figure 2-15).

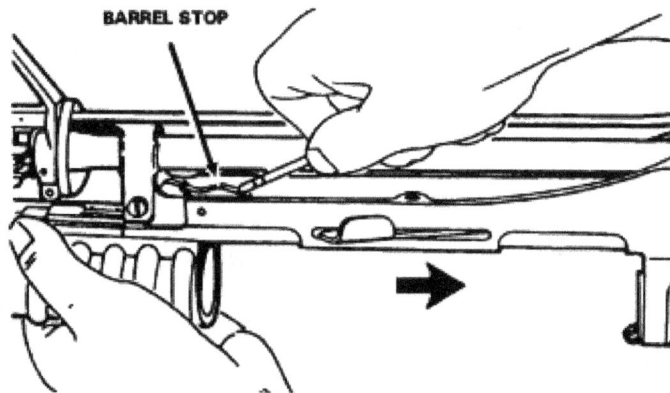

BARREL STOP

Figure 2-15 Reattaching the barrel to older M203 launchers

2. Lock the barrel by moving it rearward until it closes with a CLICK (Figure 2-16).

Figure 2-16 Locking the barrel onto the receiver

3. Install the handguard and secure it with the slip ring.

4. Install the quadrant sight assembly, hand tight only (Figure 2-17).

Figure 2-17 Tighten to the right, hand tight

Reassembling the LMT Rail Mounted M203 Grenade Launcher

The operator will assemble the grenade launcher in the reverse order that he disassembled it.

1. To install the Rail Mounted Launcher on the Picatinny rail loosen the 5/32" hex screws on the rail gripper. On M4 type rifle/carbines keep the launcher as far to the rear of the bottom rail as possible and tighten the three hex screws to hand tight with the 5/32" or Torx T-25 wrench. On AK type rifles keep the launcher approximately 8 ribs forward of the bottom rail so as to allow room for inserting and removing the AK's ammunition magazine. Test the loading and unloading of the magazine once the launcher is installed on the forearm.

2. Install the barrel by aligning the barrel assembly rail with the receiver pressing up on the barrel stop with the barrel alignment rail (there will be spring tension) and slide the barrel onto the receiver (Figure 2-18).

Figure 2-18 Aligning and reattaching the barrel onto the receiver

3. Lock the barrel by moving it rearward until it closes with a CLICK (Figure 2-19).

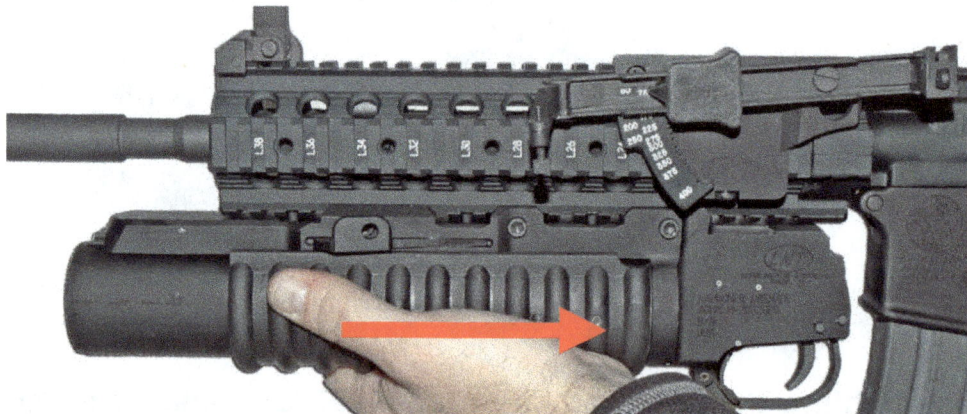

Figure 2-19 Locking the barrel onto the receiver

4. Install the quadrant sight assembly on the rear and left side of the Picatinny rail, hand tight only; flat head screwdriver is needed (Figure 2-20).

Figure 2-20 Tighten to the right, hand tight

Performing a Function Check on the M203 Grenade Launcher

Ensure the weapon is clear!

1. Check the proper operation of the sear.
   A. Cock the launcher and pull the trigger. The firing pin should release with a metallic click.
   B. Hold the trigger to the rear and cock the launcher again.
   C. Release the trigger; then pull. The firing pin should again release.

   WARNING- **If the sear malfunctions, the launcher could fire without the trigger being pulled.**

2. Check the proper operation of the safety.

   A. Cock the launcher.
   B. Place the safety on "SAFE" and pull the trigger; the firing pin should not release.
   C. Place the safety on "FIRE" and pull the trigger; the firing pin should release.

3. Check the leaf sight-assembly windage-adjustment screw for proper operation. Move the elevation adjustment screw only if the weapon has been zeroed.

4. Move the barrel forward and back to be ensure the barrel stop and barrel latch function.

Section 3

Operation and Function

Care and Handling
Certain steps must be taken before, during, and after firing to maintain the grenade launcher properly.

Before firing
- Wipe the bore dry.
- Inspect the weapon as outlined in the operator's technical manual.
- Ensure the weapon is properly lubricated.

During firing
- Periodically inspect the weapon to ensure that it is lubricated.
- When malfunctions or stoppages occur, follow the procedures outlined in Section 4.
- NOTE-- If fired into snow or mud, 40mm rounds may not hit hard enough to detonate. An undetonated round may explode when stepped on or driven over. During training in snow or mud, avoid this hazard by firing only TP rounds.
- Ensure sufficient overhead clearance exists for indirect fire. Remember that some rounds arm themselves 14 to 28 meters from the muzzle of the launcher.

CHARACTERISTICS OF FIRE

The characteristics of fire discussed in this section are defined as follows:

1. **Trajectory-** This is the curve described in space by the fired round as it travels to its target. The trajectory rises as the sights are elevated.

2. **Line of Sight-** This is an imaginary line from the gun to the target, as seen through properly adjusted sights.

3. **Ordinate-** This is the vertical distance at any point between the trajectory and the line of sight.

4. **Maximum Ordinate-** This is the greatest vertical distance between the trajectory and the line of sight; it occurs at the highest point of the trajectory.

5. **Danger Space-** This is the area where the round impact or the shrapnel from the round impact injures personnel or destroys the target.

6. **Dead Space-** This is the area(s) where personnel or targets are safe from direct-fire weapons. Ditches, depressions, and ravines are examples of dead spaces.

CLASSES OF FIRE

Fire distribution is classified three ways:

1. **With Respect to the Ground-** For the M203 grenade launcher, this class of fire refers only to plunging fire. Plunging fire occurs when firing at long ranges, from high ground to low ground, into abruptly rising ground, or across uneven terrain, resulting in a loss of grazing fire at any point along the trajectory. For example, 40mm grenades fired from the top of a hill follow an arcing trajectory and land in the valley. Figure 3-1 shows an example of plunging fire.

2. **With Respect to the Target-** This includes four ways to distribute fire (Figure 3-2):

    A. **Frontal-** Frontal fire is directed against a target's front, with the target facing or moving toward the firing position.

    B. **Flanking-** Flanking fire is directed against the target's flank.

    C. **Oblique-** Oblique fire is directed against a target moving or facing at an angle rather than directly toward or perpendicular to the gun.

    D. **Enfilade-** Enfilade fire is directed along the length of a target and may be frontal or flanking, depending on which way the target is facing.

Figure 3-1 Plunging fire

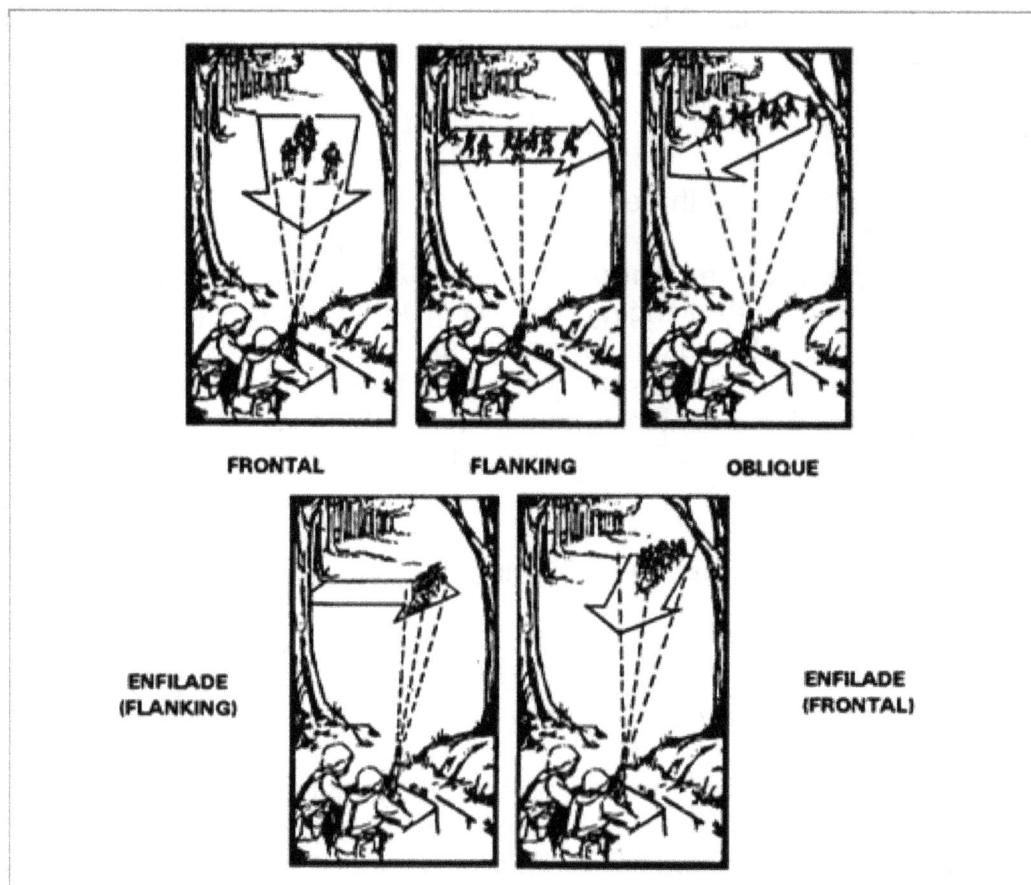

Figure 3-2 Classes of fire with respect to the target

3. **With Respect to the Weapon**- This also includes four ways to distribute fire (Figure 3-3):

    A. **Rapid Fire Point**- Distribute fire against a target with one aim point.

    B. **Rapid Fire Right or Left**- Distribute fire right to left or left to right without changing range. Use this against frontal or flanking targets.

    C. **Rapid Fire Searching**- Distribute fire against a deep target changing elevation, but not direction. Use this fire against enfilade targets.

    D. **Rapid Fire Right or Left and Searching**- Distribute fire against a target with depth and width, changing elevation and direction. Use this fire against an oblique target.

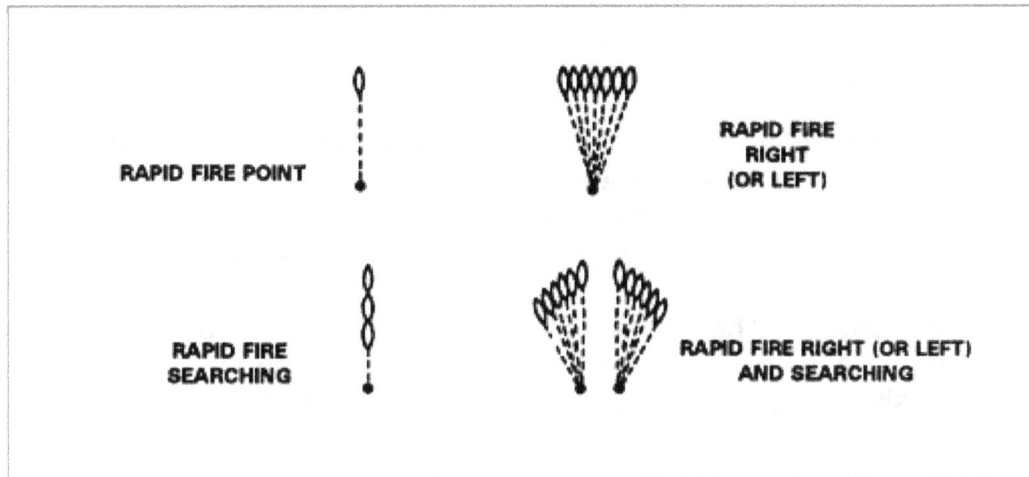

Figure 3-3 Classes of fire with respect to the weapon

RANGE ESTIMATION

The operator must be able to estimate range. This estimation enables him to hit targets with the first round and to adjust and shift fire if necessary. He often estimates range visually, using one of three methods:

1. **100-Meter Unit-of-Measurement Method**- Visualize 100 meters on the ground (this takes practice). Then estimate how many 100-meter units lie between you and the target (Figure 3-4).

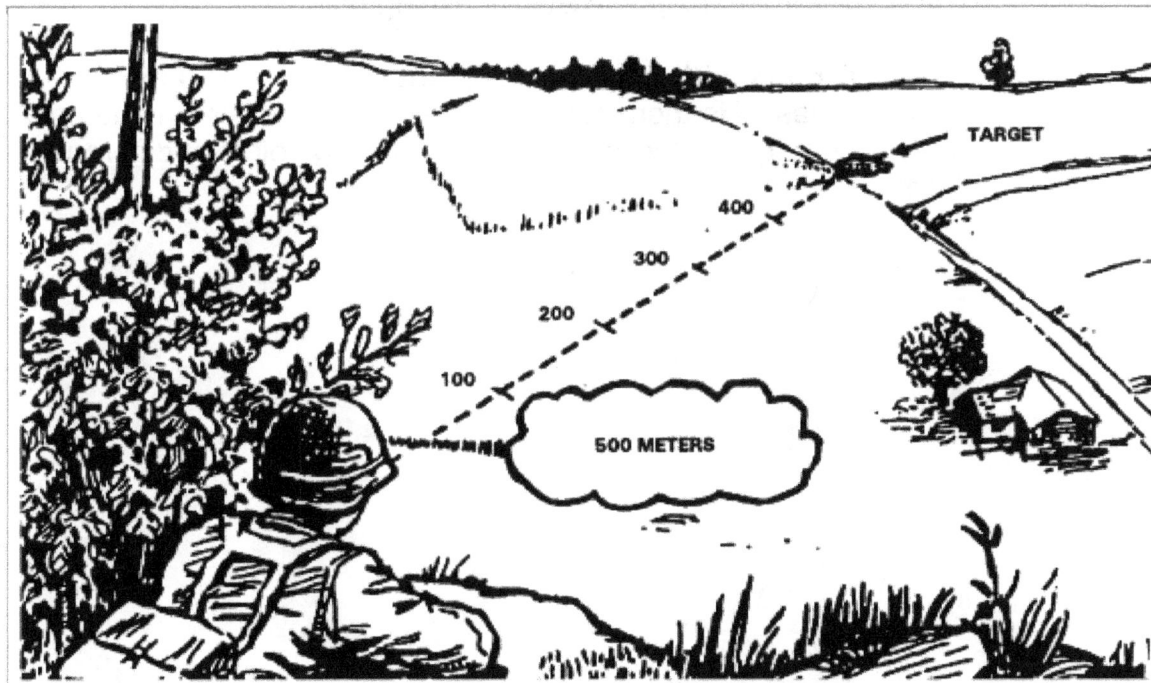

Figure 3-4 Application of the 100-meter unit-of-measurement method.

TYPES OF TARGETS

Targets for operators in combat are most likely to be enemy troops. Personnel targets have width and depth; different troop formations require different classes of fire distribution. The fire must thoroughly cover the area where the enemy is known or suspected to be, and the targets may be easy or hard to find.

1. **Point Targets**- These are targets--such as enemy bunkers, windows, weapons emplacements, light-skinned vehicles, and troops--that have a single aiming point. The maximum effective range for point targets is 150 meters.

2. **Area Targets**- These may have considerable width and depth and may require extensive right or left and searching fire. A deployed platoon is one example of an area target. The operator must know how to engage area targets regardless of their sizes or shapes. The maximum effective range for area targets is 350 meters. Types of area targets are as follows:

    A. *Linear Targets*- The operator sights on what appears to be center of mass. He fires the grenade launcher left and right across the target on successive aiming points.

    B. *Deep Targets*- The operator first lays on the center of mass of the target. He fires searching fire to the near end and then up to the far end of the target along successive aiming points.

    C. *Linear Targets with Depth*- The operator lays on the target's center of mass. He then moves the grenade launcher left and right across the target, selecting successive aiming points at different ranges.

Loading and Firing the M203 Grenade Launcher

WARNING- Keep muzzle down range and clear of all troops.

CAUTION- Before loading, make sure bore and chamber are clean and dry.

1. With the grenade launcher pointed in a safe direction, place the grenade launcher on "**SAFE**" (safety lever rearward). (Figure 3-5). If the safety cannot be positioned in the "**SAFE**" position the hammer is not cocked, open the action to cock and allow you to place the weapon on "**SAFE**".

   KEEP SAFETY IN SAFE POSITION UNTIL READY TO FIRE.

Figure 3-5 Safety is in SAFE position

2. Press barrel latch and slide barrel forward (Figure 3-6).

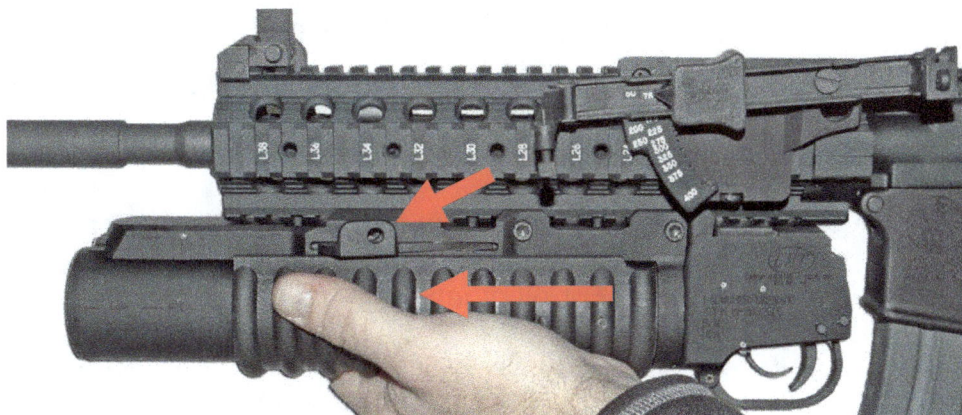

Figure 3-6 Unlocking the action

3. Insert ammunition into chamber (Figure 3-7).

Figure 3-7 Loading the cartridge into the chamber

4. Slide barrel closed until it lock "CLICKS" (Figure 3-8).

Figure 3-8 Closing the action

5. Determine target distance and select range.

   A. Launcher may be fired from standing, kneeling, or prone position. When firing long range from prone position, place stock of weapon on the ground. For all other positions, hold stock firmly against your shoulder.

   B. For short range targets, place leaf sight down and use rifle sights. Estimate distance to target and aim head high on the target.

   C. For targets from 50 to 250 meters, set and use the quadrant sight or raise leaf sight and use with rifle front sight.

Figure 3-9a Leaf Sight Alignment for 200-meter target

Figure 3-9b Quadrant Sight Alignment at desired range setting

D. With the above sight alignment, place the front sight on the target (Figures 3-9a & 3-9b).

6. Place the safety in the "**FIRE**" position.

7. Continue to aim and squeeze the trigger straight to the rear till the round fires, maintain follow through, and practice proper breath control for accurate round placement.

Unloading the M203 Grenade Launcher

1. Ensure the safety is in the "**SAFE**" position and the muzzle is pointed in a safe direction.

2. The operator must first depress the barrel latch and move the barrel forward.

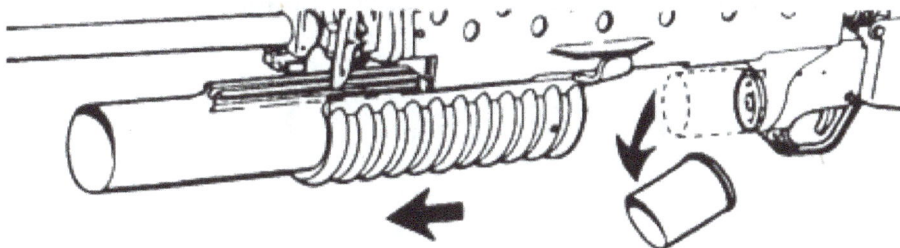

Figure 3-10a Opening the action to extract and eject spent cartridge casing

Figure 3-13a Unloading a fired grenade

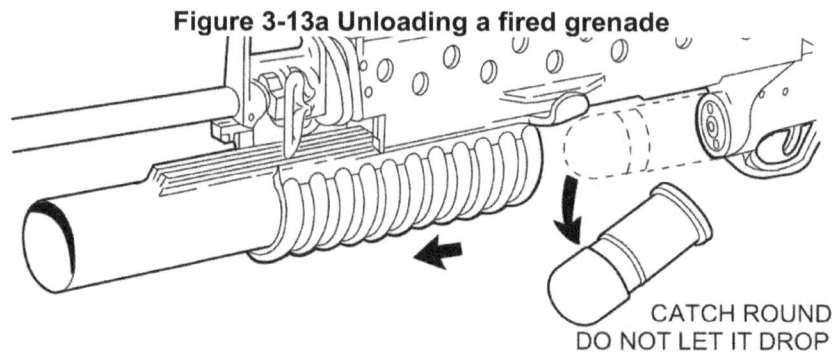

CATCH ROUND
DO NOT LET IT DROP

Figure 3-10b Unloading a live grenade

3. The round automatically extracts and ejects; if it is the casing of a fired grenade, allow it to fall clear of the receiver (Figure 3-10a). NOTE- Catch the round if it is live and do not let it drop (Figure 3-10b).

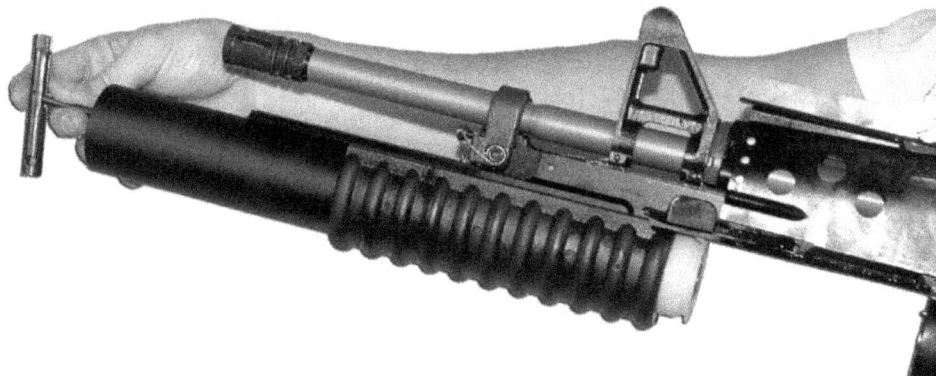

Figure 3-11 Using a cleaning rod to remove a stuck casing

4. If the case is stuck, tap it with a cleaning rod to remove it (Figure 3-11). Place the weapon on "**SAFE**", and then slides the barrel rearward, locking it to the breech.

WARNING
If you are unloading a weapon that has not been fired, avoid detonation either by catching the ejected round or by holding the weapon close to the ground to reduce the distance the round can fall.

Zeroing the M203 Grenade Launcher

A correct zero consists of the elevation and windage sight settings that enable the operator to hit the point of aim at a given range with one of the three sighting systems: leaf, quadrant, or night sight. To zero the M203 using either the leaf sight or quadrant sight, the operator engages a target at 200 meters. (The M203 is normally zeroed using only the quadrant sight, but may be zeroed with both sights or with only the leaf sight.) Do not zero in under 100 meters (330 ft).

Select a target at 200 meters (660 ft) and fire a round. If the round does not fall within 5 meters (17 ft) of target, zero the weapon as follows.

Figure 3-12 Leaf sight, example of 200 Meter shot

Leaf Sight Nomenclature

1- Elevation Adjustment Screw
2- Elevation Adjustment Increments (10 m)
3- Windage Adjustment Screw
4- Windage Adjustment Increments (1.5 m)

1. **Zeroing the Leaf Sight**. A red mark at 50 meters on the leaf sight reminds the operator not to zero at this range.

    A. Select a target at 200 meters.

    B. Place the sight in the upright position.

    C. Place the center mark of the windage scale on the index line on the rear of the sight base.

D. Loosen the elevation adjustment screw on the leaf sight.

E. Place the leaf sight's index line on the sight mount's center elevation mark.

F. Tighten the elevation-adjustment screw.

G. Assume a prone supported firing position.

H. Load one round of 40mm HE or T/P ammunition.

I. Use correct sighting and aiming procedures to align the target with the front leaf sight.

J. Fire a round, sense the impact, and adjust the sight.

    (1) *Windage.* Turn the sight windage screw clockwise to move the leaf sight to the left and vice versa. One increment moves round impact 1 1/2 meters at a range of 200 meters.

    (2) *Range.* Use a 40mm cartridge case and turn the elevation adjustment screw to raise the leaf sight (this increases range) or to lower the leaf sight (this decreases range). Turning the screw one increment moves round impact 10 meters at a range of 200 meters.

K. Fire two more cartridges, readjusting the sight after each. Once a round impacts within 5 meters of the target, the weapon is zeroed.

L. After you have zeroed the weapon, record the zero data on your data book. As soon as you can, transfer the information to a small piece of paper and tape this inside the M16 pistol grip.

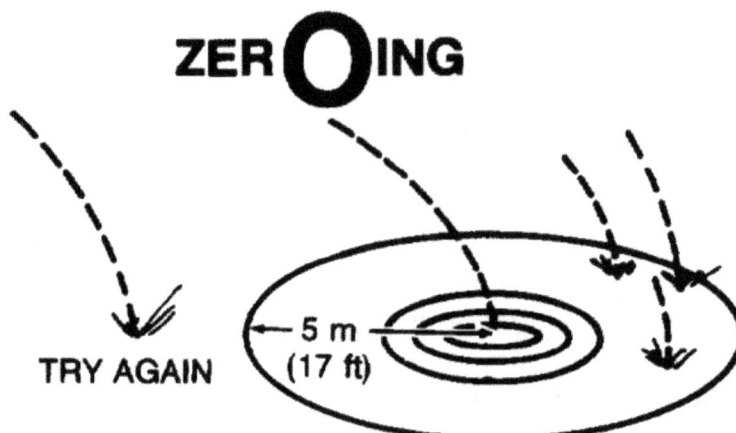

Figure 3-13 Desired size of impact area

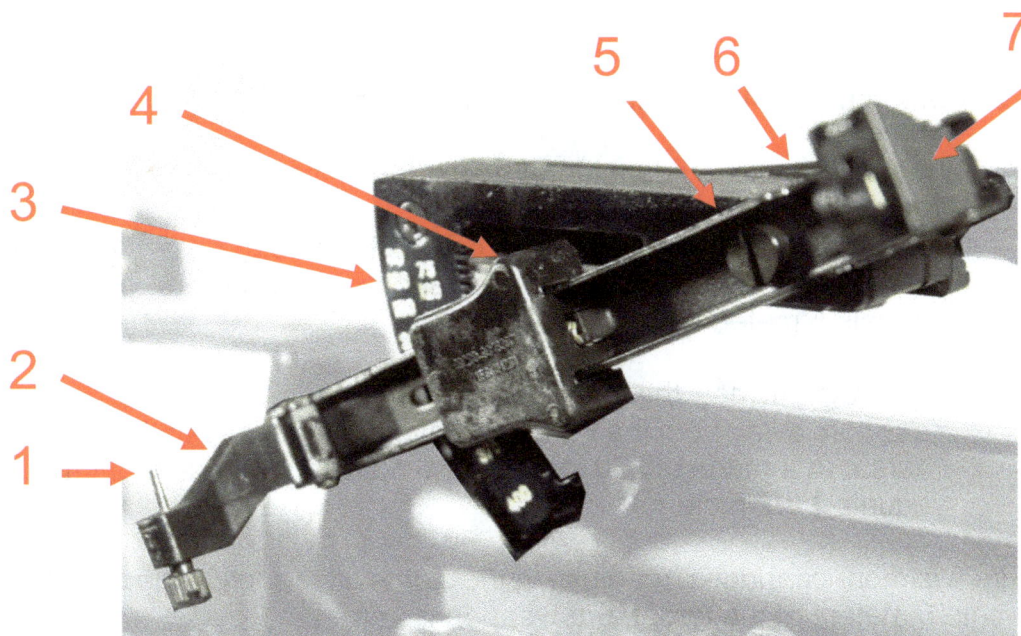

Figure 3-14 Quadrant sight

Quadrant Sight Nomenclature

1- Front Sight
2- Front Sight Post Arm
3- Range Quadrant

4- Range Adjustment Latch
5- Mounting Screw
6- Rear Sight Aperture

7- Rear Sight Arm

2. **Zeroing the Quadrant Sight**.

    A. Select a target at 200 meters.

    B. Ensure that the quadrant sight is correctly mounted on the rifle's carrying handle.

    C. Open the front sight post and rear sight aperture.

        1) Move the front sight post to its highest position and then back 2 1/2 turns.
        2) Depress the rear sight retainer. Slide the rear sight aperture to the left until its white index line aligns with the edge of the sight aperture arm.

    D. Move the sight latch rearward and reposition the quadrant sight arm to zeroing range (200 meters).

    E. Assume a prone-supported firing position.

    F. Use correct sighting and aiming procedures to align the target with the front sight post and rear sight aperture.

G. Load one round of 40mm HE or TP ammunition.

H. Fire a round, sense the impact, and adjust the sight.

    1) *Elevation.* Turn the front sight post right (to decrease elevation) or left (to increase elevation). At a range of 200 meters, one full turn equals 5 meters.

    2) *Windage.* Press the sight aperture retainer. Move the rear sight aperture away from the barrel to move the trajectory to the left or vice versa. At a range of 200 meters, one notch on the rear sight aperture equals 1 1/2 meters.

I. Fire two more cartridges, readjusting the sights after each. If the round lands within 5 meters of the target, the weapon is zeroed.

J. After you have zeroed the weapon, record the zero data on your data book. As soon as you can, transfer this information to a small piece of paper and tape this inside the M16 pistol grip.

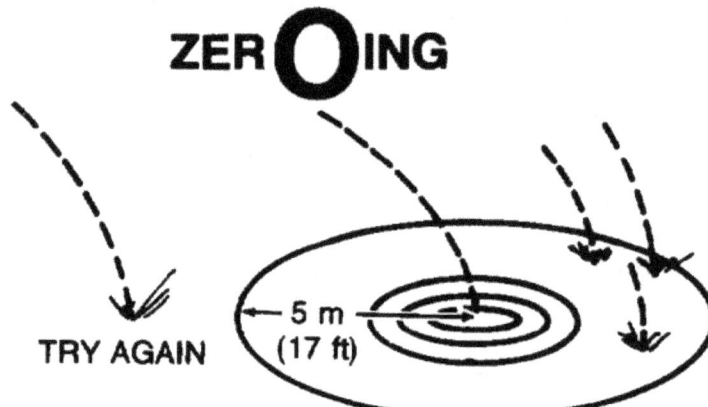

Figure 3-15 Desired size of impact area

Four Fundamentals of Marksmanship

The four fundamentals of M203 marksmanship are steady position, aiming, breathing, and trigger control. Only the first fundamental (steady position) varies. The other three remain the same regardless of the operator's position.

Steady Position- This varies according to the position and the type of sight used (quadrant or leaf).

1. **Prone Position**- When firing prone, a supported position is best.

    a. Quadrant Sight (Figure 3-16)

        i. Lie face down, grasp the M16/M4 magazine with your right hand, and place the butt of the rifle into the pocket of your right shoulder.

        ii. Lower your right elbow to the ground so your shoulders are level. This places the weight of your body behind the weapon, which enables you to recover quickly each time you fire.

        iii. Grasp the barrel grip with your left hand, supporting with sandbags. Straighten your upper body and spread your legs a comfortable distance apart. Try to point your toes outward and relax your ankles so your heels will rest on the ground. Relax the weight of your upper body forward onto your left arm.

Figure 3-16 Prone supported position, quadrant sight

    b. Leaf Sight (Figure 3-17)

        i. While firing with the leaf sight at ranges greater than 150 meters, place the butt stock of the weapon under your armpit and grip firmly to prevent the weapon from moving.

ii. Lean your head 45 degrees to the right and place the M16 front sight post on the desired range. Raise the butt stock and lower the muzzle to obtain the proper sight alignment and sight picture.

WARNING
Ensure the sling is clear of the weapon muzzle before firing.

Figure 3-17 Prone supported position, leaf sight

2. **Kneeling Position**

   a. Quadrant Sight (Figure 3-18)

      i. Kneel on your right knee while facing the target with your right hand on the magazine and your left hand grasping the barrel grip.

      ii. Place your left foot about .45 meter (18 inches) to your left front with your toes pointing in the general direction of the target.

      iii. Keeping your right toe in place, sit on your right heel.

      iv. Place your left elbow forward of your left knee, resting the flat portion of your upper arm on your knee.

      v. Move the rifle butt into the pocket of your right shoulder, pulling the rifle magazine with your right hand and grasping the barrel grip with your left hand.

      vi. With your right hand on the rifle magazine, place your right forefinger in the trigger guard of the grenade launcher.

      vii. Pull the rifle firmly into your shoulder.

viii. Pull your right elbow in close to your body to help you apply rearward pressure to the weapon. Ensure that your leg completes a solid, three-point base for your position.

Figure 3-18 Kneeling position, quadrant sight

b. Leaf Sight (Figure 3-19)

  i. For ranges greater than 150 meters, place the butt stock of the weapon under your armpit and grip firmly to prevent the weapon from moving.

  ii. Lean your head 45 degrees to the right and place the front sight post of the M16 on the desired range. Raise the butt stock and lower the muzzle to obtain the proper sight alignment and sight picture.

Figure 3-19 Kneeling position, leaf sight

3. **Sitting Position, Open-Legged**

   a. Quadrant Sight (Figure 3-20)

      i. Sit down, breaking your fall with your right hand, and slide your buttocks well to the rear. Face the target half right, and spread your feet wide.

      ii. Grasp the rifle magazine with your right hand and the barrel grip with your left hand.

      iii. Bend forward from your hips.

      iv. Move the butt of the rifle into the pocket of your right shoulder, still holding the rifle magazine with your right hand.

      v. Pull the weapon down slightly with your left hand and pull it to the rear firmly with your right hand.

Figure 3-20 Sitting position, open-legged, quadrant sight

b. Leaf Sight (Figure 3-21)

    i. For ranges greater than 150 meters, place the butt stock of the weapon under your armpit and grip firmly to prevent the weapon from moving.

    ii. Lean your head 45 degrees to the right and place the M16 front sight post on the desired range. Raise the butt and lower the muzzle to obtain the proper sight alignment and sight picture.

Figure 3-21 Sitting position, open-legged, leaf sight

4. **Sitting Position, Cross-Ankle**

   a. Quadrant Sight (Figure 3-22)

      i. Sit facing the target half right.

      ii. Extend your legs from your body and cross your left ankle over your right ankle.

      iii. Keep both ankles straight.

      iv. Grasp the rifle magazine with your right hand and the barrel grip with your left.

      v. Place your left upper arm across your left knee.

      vi. Move the butt of the rifle into the pocket of your right shoulder.

Figure 3-22 Sitting position, cross-ankle, quadrant sight

   b. Leaf Sight (Figure 3-23)

      i. For ranges greater than 150 meters, place the butt stock of the weapon under your armpit and grip firmly to prevent the weapon from moving.

      ii. Lean your head 45 degrees to the right and place the M16 front sight post on the desired range. Raise the butt and lower the muzzle to obtain the proper sight alignment and sight picture.

Figure 3-23 Sitting position, cross-ankle, leaf sight

5. **Sitting Position, Cross-Legged**

    a. Quadrant Sight (Figure 3-24)

        i. Sit down facing the target half right.

        ii. Cross your left leg over your right leg and draw both feet close to your body.

        iii. Grasp the rifle magazine with your right hand.

        iv. Move the butt of the rifle into the pocket of your right shoulder, and grasp the rifle barrel grip properly with your left hand.

Figure 3-24 Sitting position, cross-legged, quadrant sight

b. Leaf Sight (Figure 3-25)

    i. For ranges greater than 150 meters, place the butt stock of the weapon under your armpit and grip firmly to prevent the weapon from moving.

    ii. Lean your head 45 degrees to the right and place the M16 front sight post on the desired range. Raise the butt and lower the muzzle to obtain the proper sight alignment and sight picture.

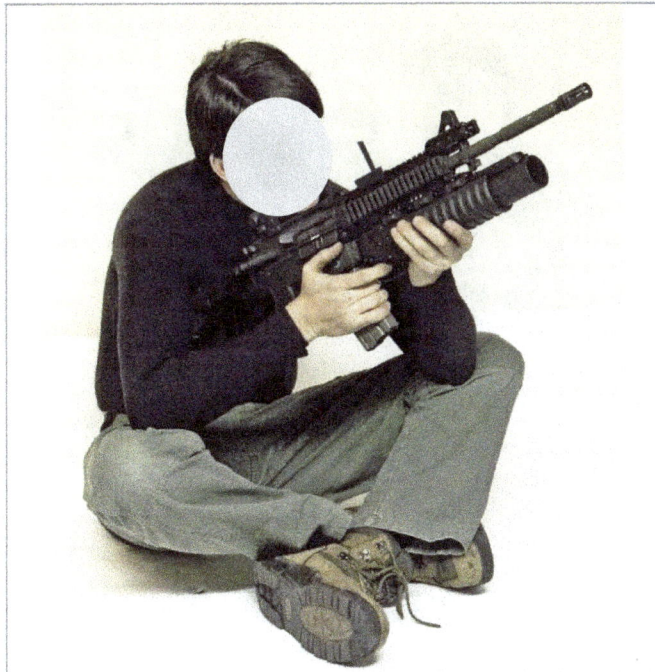

Figure 3-25 Sitting position, cross-legged, leaf sight

6. **Squatting Position**

    a. Quadrant Sight (Figure 3-26)

        i. Turn half right to the target and, keeping both feet flat on the ground and a comfortable distance apart; squat as low as you can.

        ii. Grasp the rifle magazine with your right hand.

        iii. Place your left upper arm inside your left knee and the butt of the rifle into the pocket of your right shoulder. Grasp the rifle barrel grip properly.

        iv. Lower your right elbow against the inside of your right knee.

Figure 3-26 Squatting position, quadrant sight

b. Leaf Sight (Figure 3-27)

   i. For ranges greater than 150 meters, place the butt stock of the weapon under your armpit and grip firmly to prevent the weapon from moving.

   ii. Lean your head 45 degrees to the right and place the M16 front sight post on the desired range. Raise the butt and lower the muzzle to obtain proper sight alignment and sight picture.

Figure 3-27 Squatting position, leaf sight

7. Fighting Position

a. Quadrant Sight- If possible, use support when firing from a fighting position (Figure 3-28).

   i. Place your right foot against the rear of the fighting position and lean forward until your chest is against its forward edge.

   ii. Grasp the magazine with your right hand.

   iii. Place your left elbow on or against solid support.

   iv. Use your right hand to position the butt of the rifle in the pocket of your right shoulder. Grasp the rifle barrel grip properly.

   v. Place your right elbow on or against a solid support and relax into a comfortable firing position.

   NOTE: The weapon must not touch the support.

Figure 3-28 Fighting position, quadrant sight

b. Leaf Sight (Figure 3-29)

   i. For ranges greater than 150 meters, place the butt stock of the weapon under your armpit and grip firmly to prevent the weapon from moving.

   ii. Lean your head 45 degrees to the right and place the M16 front sight post on the desired range. Raise the butt and lower the muzzle to obtain proper sight alignment and sight picture.

Figure 3-29 Fighting position, leaf sight

8. **Standing Position**

    a. Quadrant Sight (Figure 3-30)

        i. Face the target while standing with your feet spread a comfortable distance apart.

        ii. Grasp the rifle barrel grip with your left hand and the rifle magazine with your right hand.

        iii. Place the butt of the stock into your right shoulder so that the sight is level with your eyes.

        iv. Hold your right elbow high to form a good pocket for the butt of the stock and to permit a strong rearward pressure with your right hand.

        v. Hold most of the weight of the weapon with your left hand.

        vi. Shift your feet until you achieve a natural aiming stance.

Figure 3-30 Standing position, quadrant sight

b. Leaf Sight (Figure 3-31)

     i. For ranges greater than 150 meters, place the butt stock of the weapon under your armpit and grip firmly to prevent the weapon from moving.

    ii. Lean your head 45 degrees to the right and place the M16 front sight post on the desired range. Raise the butt and lower the muzzle to obtain the proper sight alignment and sight picture.

Figure 3-31 Standing position, leaf sight

Aiming. Aiming procedures for every position are as follows:

1. **Aligning Sight-** When using the leaf sight, align it with the front sight post of the M16. When using the quadrant sight, align its rear sight aperture with its front sight post. Picture a horizontal line through the center of the leaf sight or rear sight aperture; the top of the M16's front sight post should touch this line. Picture a vertical line through the center of the leaf sight or rear sight aperture: this line should vertically bisect the front sight post (Figure 3-32).

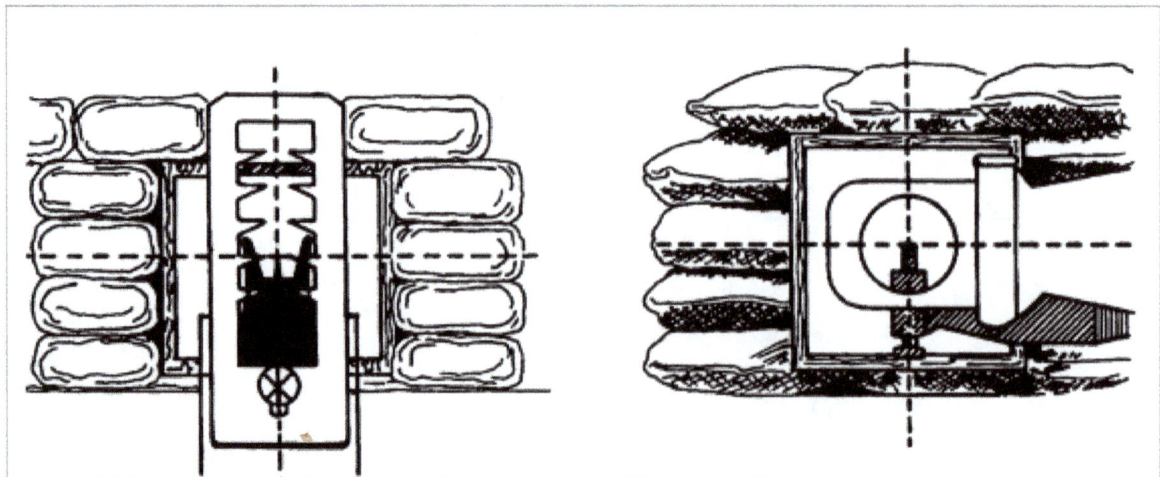

Figure 3-32 Sight pictures for leaf and quadrant sights

2. **Focusing**- For either sight, focus on the front sight post. A good firing position places your eye directly on line with the center of the leaf sight or rear sight aperture. Your eye's natural ability to center objects in a circle and seek the point of greatest light will help you align the sight correctly.

3. **Obtaining Sight Picture-** To achieve a correct sight picture, align the front sight post and the leaf sight or rear sight aperture with the target. For area targets, aim where the round's bursting radius will make the round most effective. For point targets, aim at the target's center of mass.

4. **Breathing**- The technique for breathing is the same for every position: Breathe naturally, exhale most of your air, hold your breath, and fire before you become uncomfortable. In combat, just choke off your breath before firing.

5. **Trigger Control**- The technique for trigger control is the same for every position. Place your trigger finger (the index finger of your right hand) so that the trigger is between the first joint and the tip of your finger (not at the extreme end of your finger). Adjust for your hand size and grip. Then, squeeze your trigger finger to the rear without disturbing the lay of the weapon.

Limited Visibility

The fundamentals of marksmanship are almost the same in limited visibility as in normal visibility.

A. **Steady Position**- An M203 with an AN/PVS-4 mounted on it leans to the left. When assuming a steady position, the operator must apply more rearward pressure to compensate for the lean and then steady the weapon.

B. **Aiming**- The operator sights with the reticle of the AN/PVS-4 rather than with the M203's iron sights. Sighting this way requires him to change position, which breaks his stock weld and makes the weapon seem heavier.

C. **Breathing**- Though breathing itself is affected little by limited visibility, using night vision devices that magnify the field of view increases the effect of weapon movement caused by breathing.

D. **Trigger Control**- This is the same regardless of visibility conditions. The objective is to keep the weapon aligned with the target.

E. **Night Vision Devices**- The AN/PVS-7 is issued for use with the M203, whereas the AN/PVS-4 is normally issued for use with crew-served weapons. M203 gunners may qualify with either device. In a defensive position, the gunner identifies targets during daylight and constructs aiming or elevation stakes. Because the AN/PVS-7 rear sight must be set to the far setting to sense rounds, the gunner cannot see both the M203 sights and the target at the same time. Therefore, stakes are more important with the AN/PVS-7 than with the AN/PVS-4. (On the rear sight of the M16A1, the far setting is "L." On the rear sight of the M16A2, the far setting is "02.")

F. **Marked-Sling Method**. The best field-expedient method for firing the M203 grenade launcher in limited visibility is the marked-sling method using only the M16 rifle series (Figure 3-33). To use this method, the operator must

A. Face the target and kneel on the right knee (if firing right-handed), keeping the left foot pointed toward the target.

B. Loosen the sling and place the forward foot in the sling.

C. Place the butt of the stock firmly on the ground.

D. Using the left hand, grasp firmly the upper barrel grip just below the barrel.

E. Grasp the receiver group with the right hand.

Figure 3-33 Marked-sling method

F. Ensure the sling is taut and vertical between the front sling swivel and the boot (Figure 3-34). If not, the rounds will impact at a greater range than desired.

Figure 3-34 Front-sling swivel and front of boot

G. Fire several rounds to determine the desired range.

H. Mark the sling (where it is held to the ground by the foot) with colored tape, paint, ink, or whatever is available. Mark the position of the buckles so that, if either is moved, the operator can return them to their original positions and be assured of constant range accuracy.

I. If the sling gets wet, it may stretch or shrink, indirectly causing the rounds to impact closer or farther than desired.

FIRE COMMANDS

Standard fire commands are explained to operators and are used during all subsequent gunnery training. Trainers give the appropriate elements before each dry-fire or live-fire exercise. The operator performs as directed and repeats each element as it is announced.

1. **Alert**- The trainer gives the alert as a fire mission. On hearing this, the operator loads the weapon and moves the safety lever to "**FIRE**".

2. **Direction**- The trainer gives the direction to target.

3. **Description**- The trainer describes the target, for example, BUNKER or MACHINE GUN POSITION, and the operator lays on the target.

4. **Range**- The trainer gives the (estimated) range to the target, for example, "150."

5. **Method of Fire**- The method of fire for either target is three rounds. On the basic range, operators fire at both point and area targets.

6. **Command to Open Fire**- To open fire, the trainer commands COMMENCE FIRING or AT MY COMMAND. When ready, the operator announces UP and fires or waits for the command to fire. When all operators are ready, the trainer gives the actual command to fire.

DRY-FIRE EXERCISES

Dry-fire exercises train operators in the techniques of loading, unloading, immediate action, fundamentals of marksmanship, and sight manipulation. These exercises are conducted with TP or dummy rounds. The trainer gives fire commands as appropriate.

1. **Loading and Unloading Exercise**- This trains the operator to operate and clear the weapon proficiently. Loading and unloading procedures should be practiced with dummy ammunition.

2. **Immediate Action Exercise**- This exercise is conducted with a dummy round and the basic grenade-launcher target.

    A. Load the weapon with a dummy round and aim it at one of the targets on the basic grenade launcher range.

    B. Maintain the sight picture while you pull the trigger to simulate firing.

    C. When you are informed that you have a misfire, apply misfire procedures; then continue to fire.

3. **Aiming Exercise**- This exercise requires the operator to simulate firing a dummy round at a target on the basic grenade launcher range.

    A. Maintain your sight picture throughout the firing cycle.

    B. If, after firing, you note that the sight picture has moved, then you were unsteady when you fired.

    C. After each shot, apply immediate action procedures to extract and eject the dummy cartridges. Then recock the barrel assembly.

4. **Sight Setting and Sight Changing Exercises-** These exercises train the operator to operate and adjust both quadrant and leaf sights.

    A. **Range-** Manipulate the sights to different range settings (quadrant sight, 50 to 400 meters; leaf sight, 50 to 250 meters). To learn to make fine adjustments for elevation, manipulate the sights from the minimum to the maximum setting. When you do not have time to adjust the sights, you may adjust the aiming point instead.

    B. **Windage-** Depress the rear sight aperture left and right and traverse the windage screw across the entire scale.

Sensing and Adjustment of Fire

The operator determines (senses) where the grenade landed relative to the target and then adjusts elevation and deflection.

1. **Sensing-** As soon as the grenade explodes, determine where it exploded with respect to the target. This is called "sensing" (the impact) and has two aspects: range and deviation. Because the casualty radius of the HE round is 5 meters (5 1/2 yards), determine both range and deviation to the nearest 5 meters.

2. **Range-** Sense the range as one of the following:
    A. **Short-** The grenade bursts between you and the target.
    B. **Over-** The grenade bursts beyond the target.
    C. **Target-** The grenade hits any part of the target.
    D. **Range Correct-** The grenade bursts slightly left or right of the target, but at the correct range.
    E. **Doubtful-** The grenade burst left or right of the operator, but you cannot sense the range.

3. **Deviation-** Announce a deviation sensing as either
    A. Right or left of the target, or
    B. On line with the target.

4. **Adjustment of Fire**. To ensure a second-round hit, adjust your fire by sensing the impact of the round and manipulating the sight.

    A. If time allows, whether using the AN/PVS-4 or AN/PVS-7, adjust the sights; if time is critical, adjust the point of aim instead.

    B. If the grenade lands more than 25 meters over or short of the target, adjust the range quadrant to bring the next grenade on target.

C. If the grenade explodes less than 25 meters from the target, adjust the point of aim to bring the next grenade on target.

D. If the launcher is properly zeroed, deviation errors are normally small and easily corrected by adjusting the aiming point. A wind strong enough to move the grenade out of its normal trajectory, however, increases the size of the deviation errors. After observing the effect of the wind on the strike of the grenade, compensate for the effect of the wind by aiming into it. This should help bring the next grenade on target. For example, if the grenade bursts to the left and short of the target, sense the strike of the round relative to the target, and then adjust an equivalent distance to the right and over the target to achieve a target hit. Watch the flight of the grenade to the target. This helps determine the effect of the wind on the grenade as it moves toward the target. Evaluating and compensating for the wind before firing increases your chances of achieving a first-round hit.

Section 4

Performance Problems

Malfunction, Stoppages, and Immediate Action Procedures

A malfunction occurs when a mechanical failure prevents the weapon from firing properly. Neither defective ammunition nor improper operation of the weapon by the firer is a malfunction. The weapon should be cleaned, lubricated, and retried. If it still fails to function, it should be turned in to the unit armorer. Malfunctions are usually preventable through good practices, but they may still occur out of the blue from time to time. Of course, you hope it is on the practice range, but you should treat each one as you are in a life-or-death situation. Practicing proper and effective corrective actions will allow you to be more confident in your grenade launcher handling. In stressful situations, you can become much more stressed due to an unforeseen malfunction that is easy to correct.

A stoppage is an unintentional interruption in the cycle of operation or functioning that may be cleared by immediate action. A stoppage is classified by its relationship to the cycle of functioning.

Malfunction drills must fix the problem 100% of the time (excluding a weapon stoppage—broken weapon) the first time performed. You must look at the grenade launcher and identify the problem (obviously the Grenade Launcher is not functioning as you need, so you must transition to another weapon or rectify the situation). It is a non-functioning weapon at this point—fix it.

You should always practice taking a covered position to correct malfunctions with considerations on how you operate.

The following pages in this chapter describe and detail corrective actions for the various malfunctions that may be encountered.

MALFUNCTIONS

1. FAILURE TO COCK:

Probable Cause	**Corrective Action**
A. Broken Sear	Turn in for armorer maintenance
B. Improper assembly of cocking lever	Turn in for armorer maintenance
C. Loose, broken, or missing cocking lever spring pin	Turn in for armorer maintenance

STOPPAGES

1. FAILURE TO FIRE:

Probable Cause	**Corrective Action**
A. Safety ON (safety in rear)	Place in "**FIRE**" position
B. Empty chamber	Load
C. Faulty ammunition	Reload
D. Water or excess lubricant in firing pin well	Hand cycle weapon several times to include pulling the trigger
E. Worn or broken firing pin	Turn in for armorer maintenance
F. Dirt or residue in firing pin recess	Clean
G. Weak or broken firing pin spring	Turn in for armorer maintenance

2. FAILURE TO EXTRACT:

Probable Cause	**Corrective Action**
A. Defective extractor spring or spring pin	Turn in for armorer maintenance
B. Ruptured cartridge case	

3. FAILURE TO EJECT:

Probable Cause	**Corrective Action**
A. Worn, broken, or missing ejector spring or retainer	Turn in for armorer maintenance

4. FAILURE TO CHAMBER:

Probable Cause	**Corrective Action**
A. Faulty ammunition	Reload
B. Dirty chamber	Clean bore and chamber

5. SAFETY FAILS TO STAY IN POSITION:

Probable Cause	**Corrective Action**
A. Missing spring pin or broken or worn Safety	Turn in for armorer maintenance

Immediate Action Procedures

Immediate action refers to anything a operator does to reduce a stoppage without taking time to look for the cause. Immediate action should be taken in the event of either a hangfire or misfire. Either can be caused by an ammunition defect or by a faulty firing mechanism. Any failure to fire must be considered a hangfire until that possibility is eliminated.

- A hangfire is a delay in the functioning of the round's propelling charge explosive train at the time of firing. The length of this delay is unpredictable, but in most cases, it ranges between a split second and 30 seconds. Such a delay in the functioning of the round could result from the presence of excess oil or grease, grit, sand, frost, or ice.

- A misfire is a complete failure of the weapon to fire. A misfire in itself is not dangerous, but because it cannot be immediately distinguished from a hangfire, it must be considered to be a hangfire until proven otherwise.

Because a stoppage may be caused by a hangfire, the following precautions must be observed until the round has been removed from the weapon and the cause of the failure determined:

- Keep the M203 pointed downrange or at the target and keep everyone clear of its muzzle. If the stoppage occurs during training, shout MISFIRE and clear the area of any operators not needed for the operation.

- Wait 30 seconds from the time of the failure before opening the barrel assembly to perform the unloading procedure.

- After removing the round from the receiver, determine whether the round or the firing mechanism is defective. Examine the primer to see if it is dented. If the primer is dented, separate the round from other ammunition until it can be disposed of properly. However, if the primer is not dented, the firing mechanism is at fault. Once the cause of the failure to fire has been corrected, the round may be reloaded and fired.

WARNING- If you are unloading a weapon that has not been fired, avoid detonation either by catching the ejected round or by holding the weapon close to the ground to reduce the distance the round can fall.

Remedial Action Procedure

Remedial action is any action taken by the gunner to restore his weapon to operational condition. Take remedial action only if immediate action does not remedy the problem.

Destruction Procedure

Destruction of any military weapon is necessary as a last resort to prevent the enemy from capturing or using it. This paragraph discusses planning for destruction, priorities and methods of destruction, and degree of damage. In combat situations, the commander has the authority to destroy weapons, but he must report doing so through channels.

1. **Planning**. SOPs for all teams should contain a plan for destroying equipment. Having such a plan ensures that the damage is effective enough to deny use of the equipment to the enemy. The plan must be flexible enough in its designation of time, equipment, and personnel to meet any situation.

2. **Priorities of Destruction**. When lack of time prevents them from completely destroying equipment, operators must destroy the same essential parts on all like equipment. The order in which the parts should be destroyed (priority of destruction) is as follows:
    A. Bolt assembly (M16) and breech mechanism (M203)
    B. Barrels (both M16 and M203)
    C. Sights or sighting equipment (including nightsight)
    D. Optics mount

3. **Methods of Destruction**. Equipment may be destroyed by any of several methods. The commander must use his imagination and resourcefulness to select the best method of destruction based on the facilities available. Time is usually critical. The methods of destruction are as follows:

    A. *Mechanical*. Use an axe, pick, sledgehammer, crowbar, or other heavy implement.

    B. *Burning*. Use gasoline, oil, incendiary grenades, other flammables, or a welding or cutting torch.

    C. ***Demolition***. Use suitable explosives or ammunition or, as a last resort, hand grenades.

    D. ***Disposal***. Bury essential parts, dump them in streams, or scatter them so widely that recovering them would be impossible.

4. Degree of Damage. The method of destruction used must damage equipment and essential spare parts to the extent that they cannot be restored to usable condition in the combat zone, either by repair or by cannibalization.

Appendix A - **Accessories**

There are various manufacturers offering better options to enhance the effectiveness and portability.

Accessories and products from Knights Armament

KAC 40mm M203 Grenade Launcher & 12 Ga. Masterkey

P/N: 96362 has a 10-inch Barrel
NSN: 1005-01-504-6335

12 Gauge "Masterkey" Shotgun
P/N: 96362 (Weight: 5.75 lbs.).
Also mounts to Standalone Modules.

—17.25"—

P/N: 98475 with 9-inch Barrel (NSN: 1010-01-504-5175) shown above with optional sights. (Weight: 2.75 lbs.)

KAC's 40mm M203 Grenade Launcher with KAC's Quick Detach mount gives added firepower to SR-16 Carbine or SR-16 M5 Rifle; or can be deployed "solo" by the use of KAC's Standalone Module.

(Also available P/N: 98162 w/12-inch Barrel)

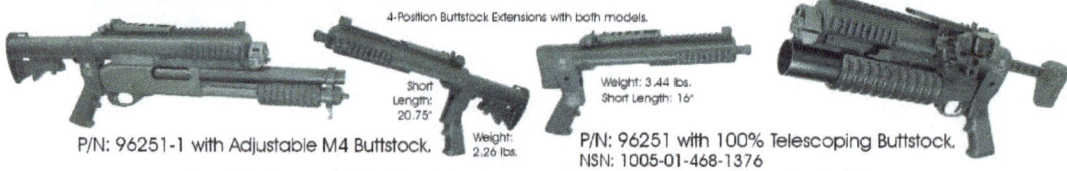

Knight's M203 quick attach-detach front mounting bracket.....P/N: 96174 NSN: 1055-01-416-1090. Over 40,000 "in Service"

4-Position Buttstock Extensions with both models.

Short Length: 20.75"
Weight: 2.26 lbs.

P/N: 96251-1 with Adjustable M4 Buttstock.

Weight: 3.44 lbs.
Short Length: 16"

P/N: 96251 with 100% Telescoping Buttstock.
NSN: 1005-01-468-1376

The KAC 40mm M203/12 Ga. Standalone Buttstock Modules P/N: 96251 & 96251-1

Improved KAC M203 Sighting Modules

MWS "Rail Grabber"
50-250 Meter Leaf Sight
Clamps to RIS or RAS Top Rail
P/N: 22109

Receiver Mounted
Reflex Quadrant Sight
Bolt's to Receiver for Optimum Zero Retention
P/N: 98370

MWS "Rail Grabber"
Reflex Quadrant Sight
Clamps to Left Rail of any RAS
P/N: 20331

Integral Rail Grabber M203 Grenade Launcher Sights
for Modular Weapon Systems (MWS)
June 05

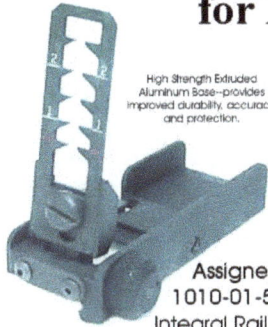

High Strength Extruded
Aluminum Base--provides
improved durability, accuracy
and protection.

Assigned NSN:
1010-01-522-0055
Integral Rail Grabber
MWS M203 Leaf Sight P/N: 22109

Specifications:
Weight: 3.65 oz.
Length: 4 inches
Range: 50-250 Meters

Attaches to Groove:
RIS: T-5
M4 RAS: T-24 / M5: T-38

When your life is on the line...
only the finest will do.

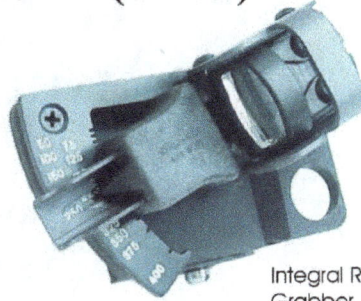

*Both sights may be
User Installed with common
flat-blade screwdrivers.*

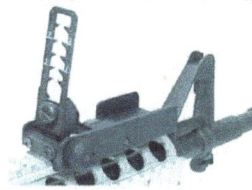

Integral Rail
Grabber
MWS M203 Reflex Quadrant
Sight P/N: 20331

Specifications:
Weight: 6.25 oz.
Length: 3.86 inches
Range: 50-400 Meters
Battery Power: 3 Volts
Attaches to Groove:
RIS: L-11   RAS: L-18

*Single 8 M.O.A. Dot Aiming Point
for rapid and accurate 1st Round Hits*

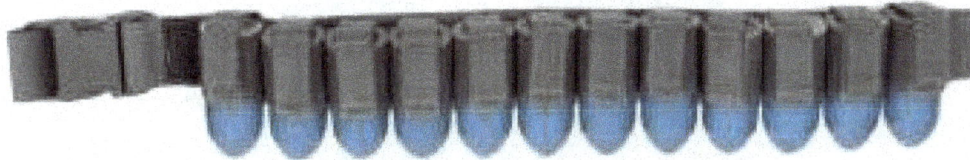

90+ "A2" Style Windage Zero
Adjustment Clicks

Standard Elevation Zero
Adjustment

Integral Rail-Grabber
Base Protects leaf
in down position

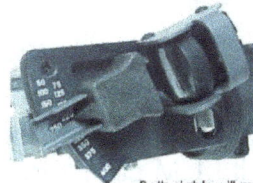

Both sights will mount simultaneously on RIS or RAS

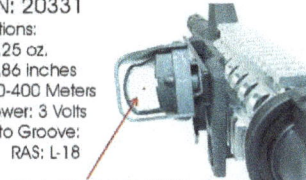

40mm Ammunition Belt by Tactical Tailor

This belt will securely hold 12 rounds of any 40mm ammunition designed for use with the M203 or other 40mm grenade launchers. The belt has 12 loops for rounds, it will hold HE, DP, Buckshot, Illumination or TP rounds. The belt can be worn around the waist or slung over the shoulder. It is available in Black, Tan, and Foliage Green. One size fits all.

BlackHawk Omega Operator 40 mm/Rifle OD Green (BH-30VT29)

The BlackHawk Omega Tactical Operator 40MM / Rifle Vest is designed to carry (8) eight 40MM HE or ILLUM canisters in pouches with adjustable lids and up to (6) M-16 or (3) AK or (3) M-14 mags. (Also fits MK-13 Flares). Wt: 3 lbs 4.8 oz.

BlackHawk S.T.R.I.K.E. Gen-4 MOLLE System 40MM Grenade Pouch (BH-37CL23)

BlackHawk S.T.R.I.K.E. 40MM Grenade Pouch, Holds 3 Grenades

Appendix B - Ammunition

Types, Characteristics and Capabilities of Ammunition used with the M203 Grenade Launcher.

The most commonly used ammunition for the M203 is the M406 antipersonnel round, which has a lethal radius of five meters, and the M433 multi-purpose round which, in addition to having fragmentation effects, will penetrate up to 3 in. (7.6 cm) of armor plate. Many other types of ammunition are available, such as buckshot, tear gas, and various signal rounds, which greatly increase the versatility of this outstanding weapon.

WARNING
- The 40mm grenades used in the M203 (40 x 46mm) are not the same as in the Mk 19 grenade launcher (40 x 53mm), which are fired at a higher velocity.
- All issued grenades must be inspected for faults- dents and cracks.
- Do not fire ammunition not made for use In the M203 grenade launcher. Doing so will result in injury to, or death of, personnel.
- If fired into snow or mud, 40mm rounds may not hit hard enough to detonate. An undetonated round may explode when stepped on or driven over. During training in snow or mud, avoid this hazard by firing only TP rounds.
- If ammunition fails to fire in your weapon, turn it in to unit armorer for disposition.
- Do not fire Pyrotechnic Ammunition made for the AN-M8 pyrotechnic pistol in the M203 Grenade Launcher. It is very dangerous.
- Make sure you have the right ammunition!
- Never load aircraft ammunition M384 (HE) or M385 (practice). You may blow your head off.

Packaging

Typically HE, HEDP, and TP are shipped in wooden boxes containing 2 metal ammo cans, with 3 bandoleers of 6 rounds each for a total of 18 rounds per metal ammo, and 36 rounds per wooden box.

Combat Load

The recommended minimum combat load is 18 rounds of the 40mm ammunition.

Cartridges for the M203 grenade launcher

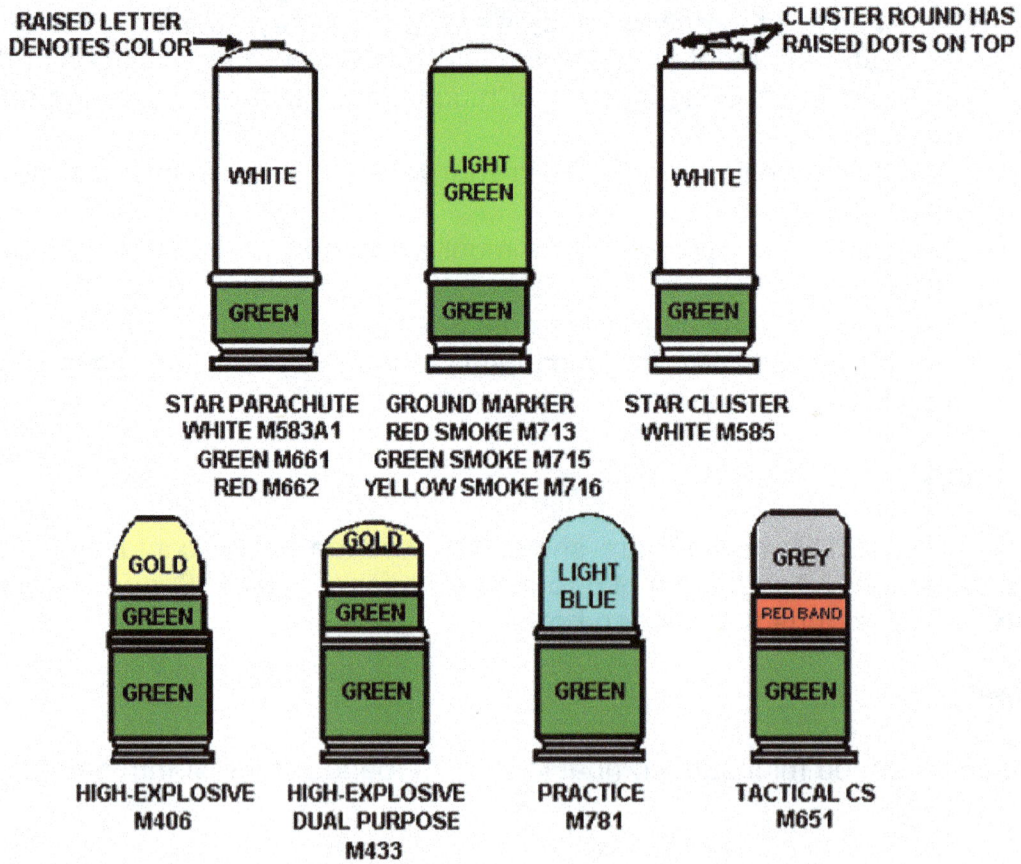

RAISED LETTER
DENOTES COLOR

CLUSTER ROUND HAS
RAISED DOTS ON TOP

STAR PARACHUTE
WHITE M583A1
GREEN M661
RED M662

GROUND MARKER
RED SMOKE M713
GREEN SMOKE M715
YELLOW SMOKE M716

STAR CLUSTER
WHITE M585

HIGH-EXPLOSIVE
M406

HIGH-EXPLOSIVE
DUAL PURPOSE
M433

PRACTICE
M781

TACTICAL CS
M651

Figure B-1 Various cartridges available for the M203

High-Explosive Dual Purpose Round, M433. The HEDP round has an olive drab aluminum skirt with a steel cup attached, white markings, and a gold ogive (head of the round). It penetrates at least 5 cm (2 in.) when fired straight at steel armor at 150 meters or less, or, at a point target, it arms between 14 and 27 meters, causes casualties within a 130-meter radius, and has a kill radius of 5 meters.

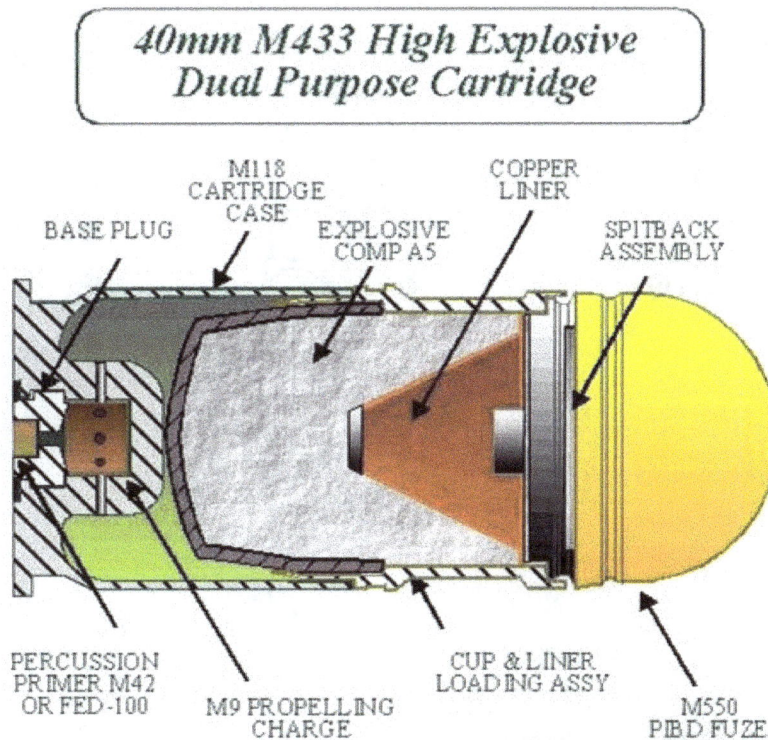

40mm M433 High Explosive Dual Purpose Cartridge

HEDP ROUND, M433
DODAC 1310-B546

LENGTH
10.29 CM (4.05 IN)

WEIGHT
0.23 KG (0.51 LB)

Figures B-2 M33 HEDP

High-Explosive Round, M406. The HE round has an olive drab aluminum skirt with a steel projectile attached, gold markings, and a yellow ogive. It arms between 14 and 27 meters, produces a ground burst that causes casualties within a 130-meter radius, and has a kill radius of 5 meters.

HE ROUND, M406
DODAC 1310-B566

LENGTH
9.89 CM (3.89 IN)

WEIGHT
0.23 KG (0.51 LB)

GOLD

GREEN

GREEN

Figure B-3 M406 HE

84

www.vig-sec.com

40-MM AMMUNITION PYROTECHNIC SIGNAL AND SPOTTING ROUNDS

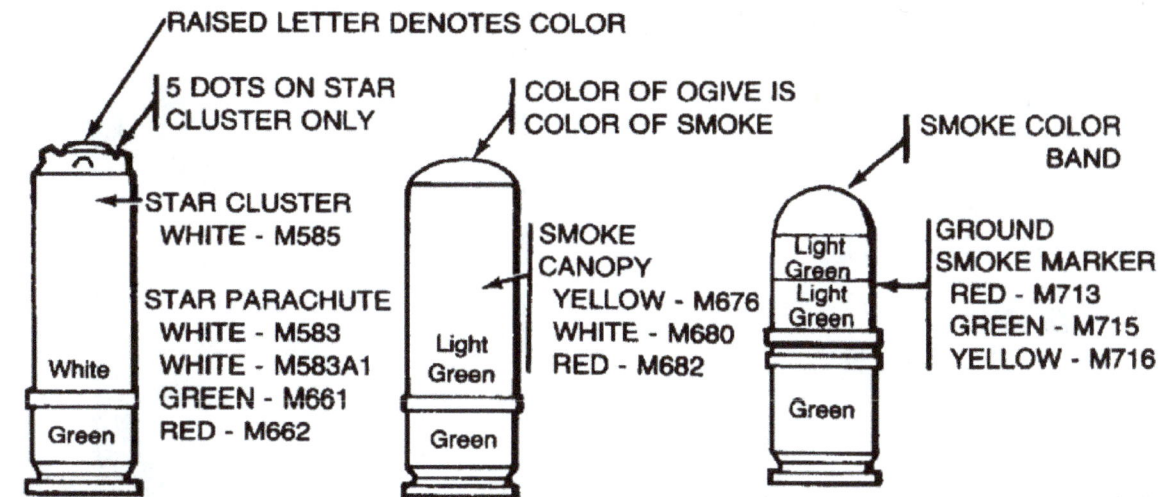

Figure B-4 Pyrotechnic signal

White Star Cluster Round, M585. This round is white impact or bar aluminum alloy with black markings. The attached plastic ogive has five raised dots for night identification. The round is used for illumination or signals. It is lighter and more accurate than comparable handheld signal rounds. The individual stars burn for about 7 seconds during free fall.

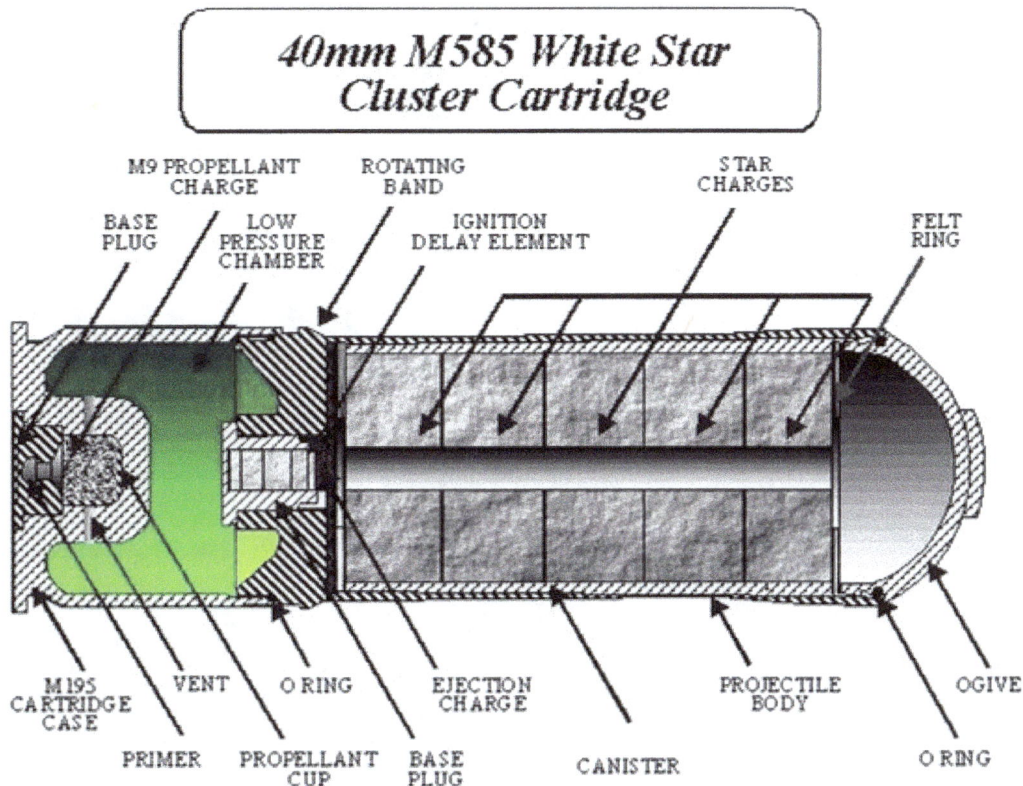

Figure B-5 M585 White Star Cluster, cutaway

STAR CLUSTER ROUND

WHITE, M585
DODAC 1310-B536

LENGTH
13.38 CM (5.27 IN)

WEIGHT
0.19 KG (0.41 LB)

Figure B-6 M585 White Star Cluster

Star Parachute Round- M583A1 (White), M661 (Green), M662 (Red), XM992 (Infrared). This round is white impact or bar alloy aluminum with black markings. It is used for illumination and signals and is lighter and more accurate than comparable handheld signal rounds. The parachute attached to the round deploys upon ejection to lower the candle at 7 feet per second. The candle burns for about 40 seconds. A raised letter on the top of the round denotes the color of the parachute.

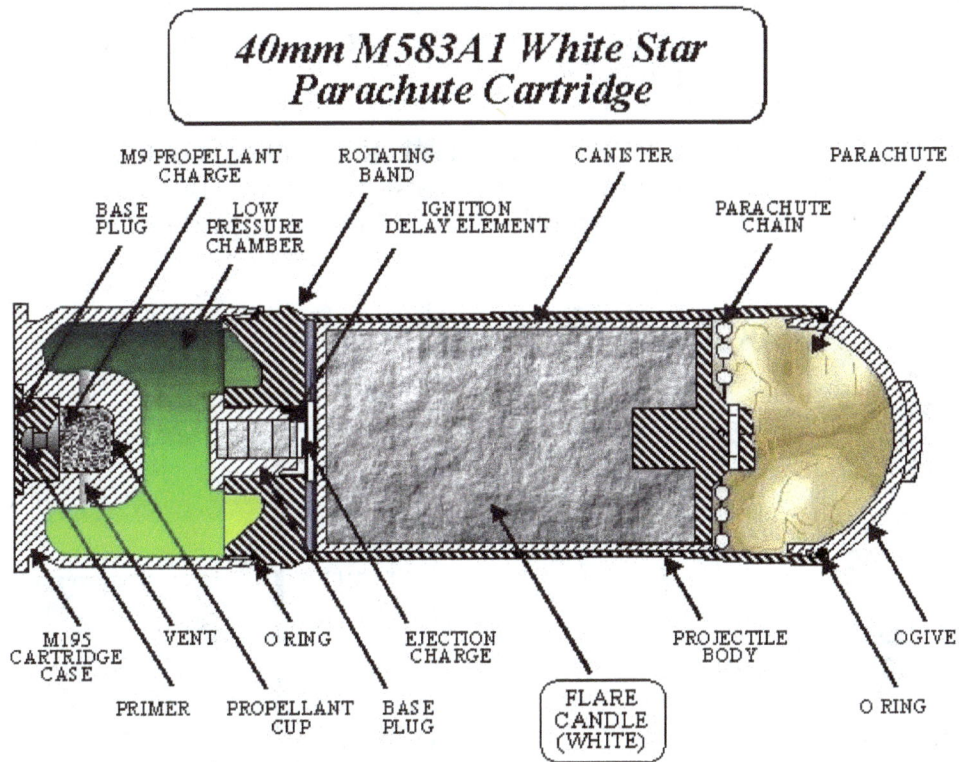

Figure B-7 M583A1 White Star Cluster, cutaway

STAR PARACHUTE ROUNDS

WHITE, M583A1
DODAC 1310-B534
90,000 CANDLEPOWER

GREEN, M661
DODAC 1310-B504
8,000 CANDLEPOWER

RED, M662
DODAC 1310-B505
20,000 CANDLEPOWER

LENGTH
13.39 CM (5.27 IN)

WEIGHT
0.22 KG (0.49 LB)

Figure B-8 Star Parachute

Ground Marker Round- M713 (Red), M715 (Green), M716 (Yellow). This round is light green impact aluminum with black markings. The color of the ogive indicates the color of the smoke.

The round is not for screening. It is used for aerial identification and for marking the location of soldiers on the ground. If a fuze fails to function on impact, the output mixture provided in the front end of the delay casing backs up the impact feature.

GROUND MARKER (SMOKE) ROUNDS

RED, M713
  DODAC 1310-B506

GREEN, M715
  DODAC 1310-B508

YELLOW, M716
  DODAC 1310-B509

LENGTH
  9.93 CM (3.91 IN)

WEIGHT
  0.22 KG (0.49 LB)

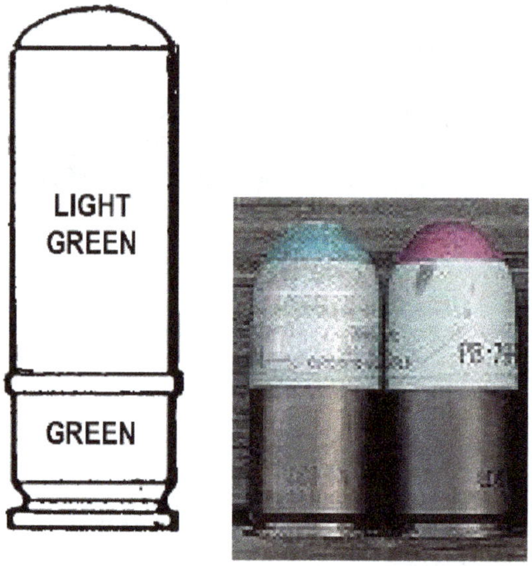

LIGHT GREEN

GREEN

Figure B-9 Smoke

The round consists of a cartridge case, a projectile with pyrotechnic smoke payload, and a pyrotechnic impact fuze.

1. The **cartridge case** is a dual-chambered aluminum container housing a brass propellant cup. The propellant cup is held in the case by a crimped base plug which provides a pressure-type waterproof seal.
2. The **projectile** utilizes a one-piece, aluminum body-ogive and a steel base. The payload consists of a pyrotechnic smoke mixture pressed into the body ogive with a cylindrical cavity in the center.
3. The **fuze** is cemented to the base of the projectile and protrudes into cylindrical cavity of the smoke mixture.

The muzzle velocity is expected to be approximately 254 fps (77 mps) and the maximum range is 437 yards (400 m).

Operation:
1. Upon firing, the primer ignites the propellant charge. In addition to launching the projectile, propellant gases ignite the first fire mixture of the fuze in base

of the projectile. The first fire mixture ignites a high temperature transfer mixture contained in the steel cup. The transfer mixture burns during the first 15 meters of projectile flight.

2. When the projectile is between 15 and 45 meters from the launcher muzzle, heat transfer through the steel cup ignites the delay mixture.

3. Upon impact, the delay casing breaks and the burning portion flies forward out of the fuze support, contacting and igniting the pyrotechnic smoke mixture.

4. Ignition of the smoke mixture causes a buildup of pressure that dislodges the fuze support at the aft end of the projectile, thus allowing smoke to be emitted at the aft end of the projectile.

5. Projectile impact prior to the minimum arming distance (15 meters) results in a dud. Between 15 and 45 meters from the launcher muzzle, the fuze may or may not function upon impact.

6. In the event that the fuze fails to function upon impact, the output mixture provided in the front end of the delay casing acts as a backup to the impact feature. When the flame reaches this point (8 to 10 seconds after launch), the output mixture flashes and ignites the smoke mixture.

Thermobaric Grenade, XM1060

The XM1060 40mm Thermobaric Grenade, developed and fielded by Picatinny Arsenal within a four-month span, is the very first small arms thermobaric device released to a US war theatre. It is applauded as a critical tool for military operations in urban terrain and close-quarters cave applications.

Thermobaric cartridges provide operators with a significantly greater probability of kill/incapacitation within the effective radius. The lethality effect results from a thermobaric overpressure blast rather than fragmentation. As a result of the thermobaric reaction, all enemy personnel within the effective radius will suffer lethal effects as opposed to the conventional fragmentation round.

In order to meet the short deadline, it was decided to use existing 40mm ammunition components. The 40mm 550 fuze, the M195 cartridge case, and a modified version of the M583 projectile body were used, along with an YJ-05 thermobaric mix (a proprietary mix from contractor Ensign Bickford).

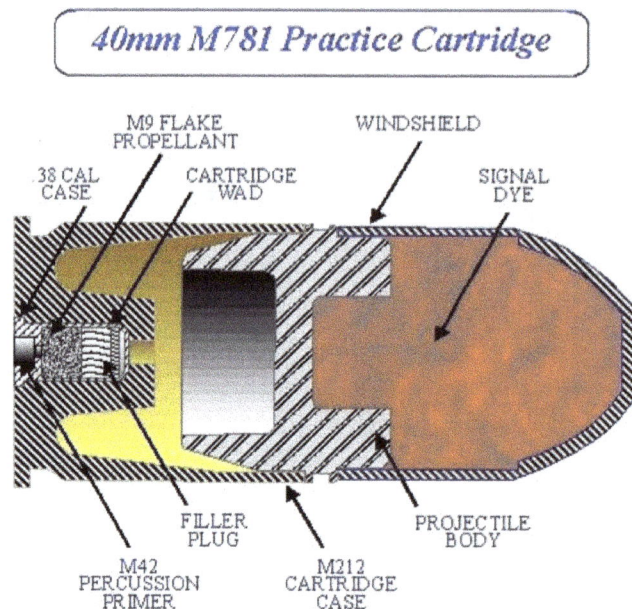

40mm M781 Practice Cartridge

Figure B-10 M781 Practice, cutaway

Practice Round, M781. Used for practice, this round is blue zinc or aluminum with white markings. It produces a yellow or orange signature on impact, arms between 14 and 27 meters, and has a danger radius of 20 meters. The M781 is a low-cost, unfuzed, fixed-round of practice ammunition ready for use as issued. The cartridge case is made of plastic material and the projectile is also plastic with an aluminum-rotating band. The ogive is made of a frangible plastic material and contains a colored dye in granular form, the consistency of talcum powder, which is used to generate a signature. The propulsion system consists of a standard .38 caliber blank.

PRACTICE ROUND, M781
DODAC 1310-B518

LENGTH
  10.29 CM (4.05 IN)

WEIGHT
  0.22 KG (0.48 LB)

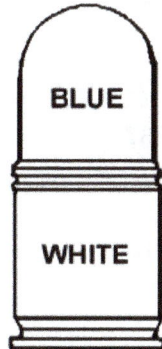

Figure B-11

Training/Practice (TP) Round, M918. Used for practice, this round is blue zinc or aluminum with white markings. It produces a yellow or orange signature on impact, arms between 14 and 27 meters, and has a danger radius of 20 meters.

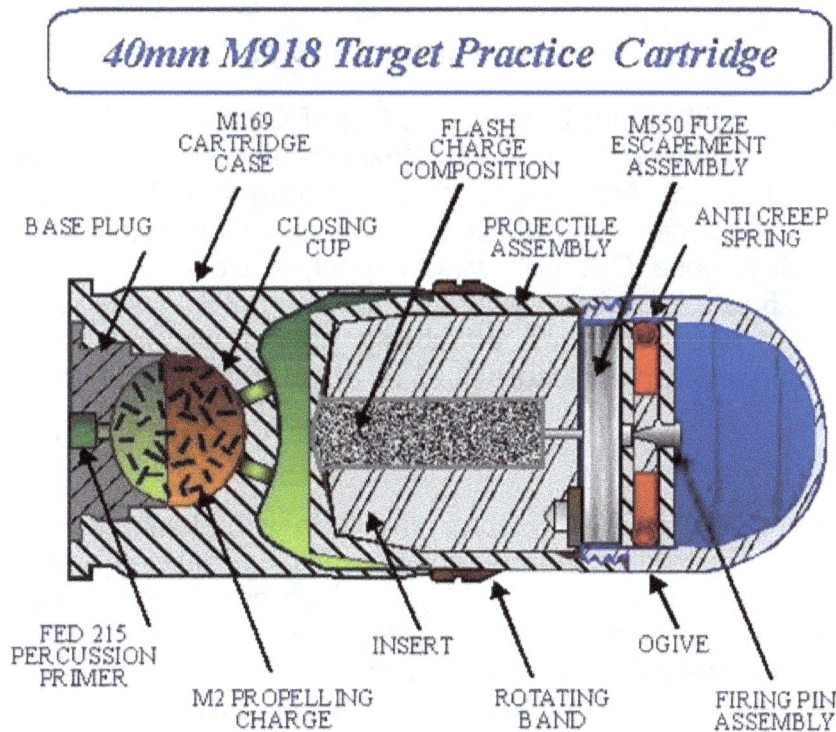

Figure B-12 M918 Target/Practice, cutaway

CS Round, M651. This round is gray aluminum with a green casing and black markings. Though it is a multipurpose round, it is most effective for riot control and in Military Operations in Urban Terrain (MOUT). It arms between 10 and 30 meters and produces a white cloud of CS gas on impact. This round is gray aluminum with a green casing and black markings.

TACTICAL CS ROUND, M651
DODAC 1310-B567

LENGTH
11.43 CM (4.50 IN)

WEIGHT
0.22 KG (0.48 LB)

Figure B-13 M651 Tactical CS

The round is filled with about 2 ounces (57 g) of CS pyrotechnic mix containing approximately 0.75 ounces (21 g) of CS. Maximum accuracy is obtained at ranges up to 219 yards (200 m). Area targets may be engaged up to 437 yards (400 m). This projectile can penetrate window glass or up to 3/4 inch-thick pine at 200 meters and still release CS. Following impact, a cloud of CS is emitted for approximately 25 seconds. Area coverage: approximately 144 square yards (120 square meters). Two cartridges effectively placed will incapacitate 95% of unmasked personnel in an enclosure of 15 by 30 by 20 feet within 60 seconds after functioning.

Buckshot Round, M576. This round is olive drab with black markings. Though it is a multipurpose round, it is most effective in thick vegetated areas or for room clearing. Inside it has at least 2,000 pellets, which cast a cone of fire 30 meters wide and 30 meters high and travel at 269 meters per second. Be sure to aim buckshot rounds at the foot of the target. The round has no mechanical-type fuse. Photo shows them in the molded plastic carry case.

Figure B-14 M576 Buckshot

Non-Lethal Round, M1006. This round incapacitates a targeted individual with Non-Lethal Blunt Trauma from 15-30 meters and provides a non-lethal means of crowd control. The non-lethal 40mm cartridge provides friendly forces with the capability to stop, confuse, disorient, or momentarily deter a potential threat without using deadly force. Military forces use this non-lethal cartridge to apply the minimum force necessary while performing missions of crowd control and site and area security of key facilities throughout the world. The non-lethal 40mm cartridge is intended to be a direct-fire, low-hazard, non-shrapnel-producing device which will produce less than lethal trauma upon impact.

The 40mm-sponge grenade provides temporary incapacitation through blunt trauma. It provides a tactical alternative for dealing with low-intensity conflicts, peacekeeping missions, and humanitarian relief missions. The projectile consists of a foam rubber nose and a high-density, plastic projectile body fired from the 40mm M203 or M79 Grenade Launchers. Minimum engagement range is 10 - 15 meters, and maximum effective range is 50 meters. Velocity at 50 meters is 200 feet per second. Also available are reload kits. Each kit consists of shell cases, rotating bands, and foam ogives in quantities of 48, 72, 96 and 120 shot quantities. These kits are for training purpose only.

Available from www.vig-sec.com

Muzzle Velocity-	76m/s (250f/s)
Effective Range-	27.4m (30 yards)
Projectile Weight-	60gm (1.192oz)
Overall Weight-	100g (3.5oz)

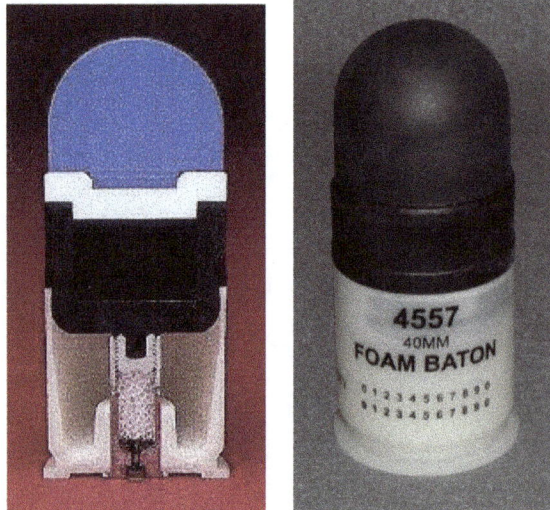

Figures B-15 BH-CTS-4557

CTS Sting Ball Cartridge (Like a Crowd Dispersal Round [Area], M1029)

The 40mm Sting Ball™ rubber pellet cartridge is designed to be skip fired in situations where collateral damage and serious injury to innocent bystanders is to be avoided. All our cartridge cases are made of aluminum alloy. These cartridges were developed specifically for 40mm grenade launchers such as the U.S. M203, M79, and the CTS TGL-1. The cartridge case fully chambers in such launchers, eliminating the possibility of the cartridge slipping past the extractor, as may occur with undersized cartridges. The undercut at the cartridge base further ensures reliable extraction after every shot. Available in .31 or .60 caliber sting balls.

The Less Lethal Crowd Dispersal Cartridge is a direct fire, low-hazard, non-shrapnel-producing projectile 40mm non-lethal cartridge effective for crowd dispersions or routing of individuals in crowd control or civil disturbance situations and against subjects who offer violent resistance. The round is extremely effective against individuals in a violent mindset or armed with impact or edged weapons. It is also effective against rioters and in rescue or street-clearing operations.

BH-CTS-4553 (.31 Caliber Balls)   BH-CTS-4558 (.60 caliber balls)

Although non-lethal ammunition is designed to help control a hostile individual or crowd without serious injury or death to targeted individuals, such instances may still occur even when non-lethal munitions are properly employed. Engaging targets at less than 10 meters greatly increases the potential lethality of this munition.

The payload spreads out from the barrel to cover an area equal to five standard E-type silhouettes standing side by side at a range of 30 meters. Be aware of possible bounce-back if fired at a wall or hard object within 20 meters of the user.

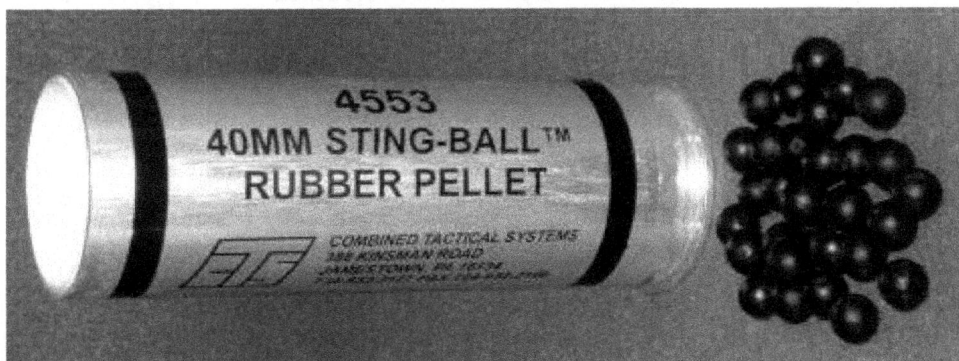

Figure B-16

40mm Kinetic Less-Lethal Rounds

CTS manufacture a complete line of 40mm less-lethal impact munitions, cartridges with rubber foam or hardwood batons. All our cartridge cases are made of aluminum alloy. Wood batons are coated and sealed with lacquer to prevent swelling through moisture absorption. These cartridges were developed specifically for 40mm grenade launchers such as the US M203, M79, and the CTS TGL-1. The cartridge case fully chambers in such launchers, eliminating the possibility of the cartridge slipping past the extractor, as may occur with undersized cartridges. The undercut at the cartridge base further ensures reliable extraction after every shot.

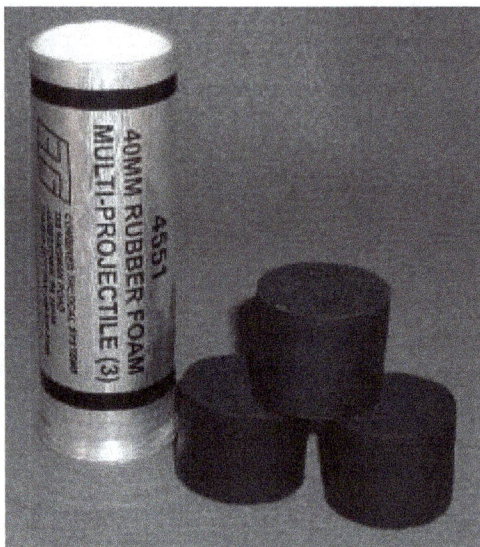

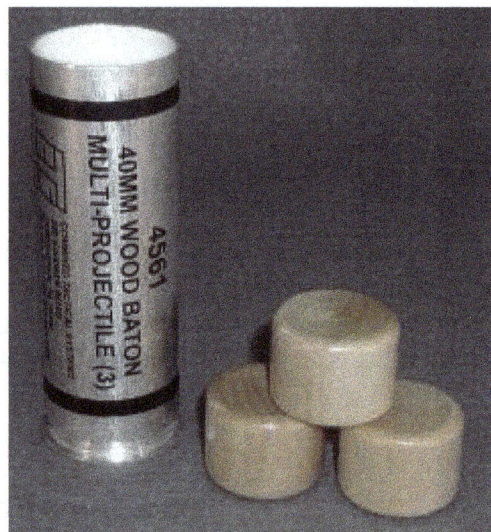

BH-CTS-4551 (Foam Baton)   **BH-CTS-4561 (Wood Baton)**
Figure B-17 CTS Baton Projectiles

40mm Liquid & Powder Barricade Projectiles

Developed specifically for rifled grenade launchers such as the US M203 and our TGL-1, these cartridges shoot projectiles that engage the barrel rifling. As a result the projectiles are spin stabilized and therefore highly accurate. The propelling system is based on the one used in the US M781 40mm practice round and uses an M212 high- and-low-pressure chamber cartridge case. This proven design keeps reliability high and costs low. The round is available in CN tear agent, CS riot control agent, OC and inert for training purposes in the liquid munitions, and CS, OC, and inert in the powder munitions. Since no fins are required for stabilization, the total of the projectile length can be used to contain agent.

The impact during target penetration ruptures a weakened circular section in the projectile nose, releasing the payload. The violent deceleration coupled with the spin instantly produce a large volume of either aerosol mist or a fine powder inside the target.

Effective Range- 45m (50 yards)
Muzzle Velocity- 122m/s (400f/s)
Overall Weight- 150gm (5.3oz)
Overall Height- 122mm (4.8")

Available in-
BH-CTS-4300 Inert Liquid Barricade   **BH-CTS-4401 Inert Powder Barricade**
BH-CTS-4320 CN Liquid Barricade   **BH-CTS-4431 CS Powder Barricade**
BH-CTS-4330 CS Liquid Barricade   **BH-CTS-4441 OC Powder Barricade**
BH-CTS-4340 OC Liquid Barricade

Figure B-18

40mm Pyrotechnic Smoke Cartridge

These cartridges were developed specifically for 40mm grenade launchers such as the US M203 and our TGL-1. The cartridge case fully chambers in such launchers, eliminating the possibility of the cartridge slipping past the extractor, as may occur with undersized cartridges. The undercut at the cartridge base further ensures reliable extraction after every shot. These rounds are available in CN tear agent, CS riot control agent, and white smoke for screening and tactical purpose. Smoke is emitted from ports at both ends of the projectile.

Effective Range-   100m (110 yds)
Overall Weight-   235gm (8.3oz)
Overall Length-   122mm (4.8")

Available in-
BH-CTS-4210 Inert Smoke
BH-CTS-4220 CN Smoke
BH-CTS-4230 CS Smoke

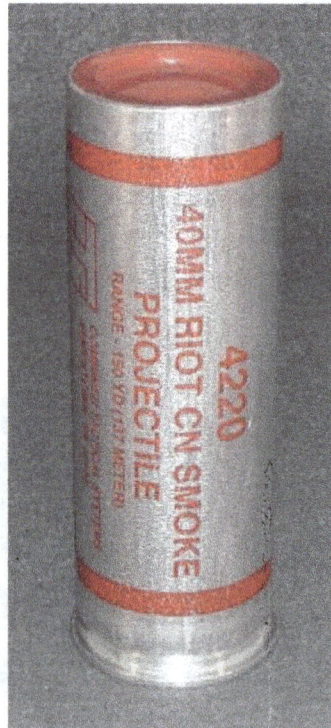

Figure B-19 BH-CTS-4220

40mm Spin-Stabilized Flash-Bang Projectile

The Model 4090 is designed for use in 40mm rifled launchers such as the M203, M79, and our TGL-1. The round uses the proven M212 cartridge case for propulsion. The flash-charge payload is contained in a rubber and plastic projectile, which is spin-stabilized for accuracy. The flash charge is initiated by a pyrotechnic delay. Dual in-line delays are used for safety.

This round provides a loud report and a bright flash 328 meters downrange. The resulting rubber and plastic fragments are low in kinetic energy and present a low risk of injury. Ballistic and timing accuracy enable precise placement of single shots or multiple shot patterns. This round is especially effective when used in conjunction with the CTS TGL-6 six-shot rotary magazine launcher.

Effective Range-	300m (330 yds)
Sound Output-	175db @ 1.52m (5')
Light Output-	6-8 million candelas, 8.5 milliseconds
Overall Weight-	120gm (6.9oz)
Overall Length-	122mm (4.8")

Available in-
BH-CTS-4090

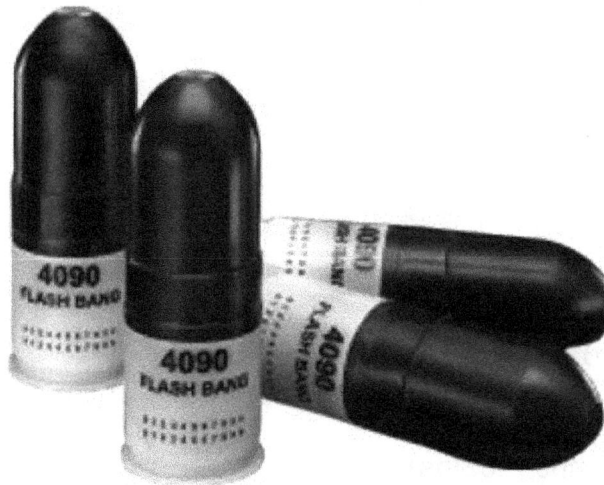

Figure B-19 BH-CTS-4090

HELLHOUND (High Order Unbelievably Nasty Destructive Series)
40MM LV Multi-Purpose Grenade

The **HELLHOUND** 40mm Low-Velocity Multi-Purpose Grenade is a fixed type ammunition designed to be fired from a 40mm Grenade Launcher M79, M203, (attached to the M16/M16A1/M16A2 rifle) or Milkor MGL-140. The round consists of an A5-filled metal projectile body with a rotating band, a point initiating-base detonating fuze with Safe and Arm technology, and a cartridge case assembly. Upon impact with the target, the firing pin is driven into the detonator, which in turn initiates the spit back charge, producing a jet which initiates the explosive train from the base forward, resulting in an armor-piercing jet of molten metal and fragmentation of the projectile body. With twice the fill amount of an M433 and a 40% increase in the shrapnel pattern and a casualty radius out to **10 meters**, the **HELLHOUND** provides superior performance against both Troops in the Open and MOUT-type engagements and **unsurpassed door breaching capabilities!**

Figure B-20 Hellhound

HELLHOUND

Technical Information
Type- HEDP
Fuze- SF801/M550
Charge- A5
Body Material- Steel
Weight- 225 grams (98 grams A5)
Length- 110mm
Weapons- M79, M203, Milkor MGL-140 launchers
Penetration- 90mm mild steel at normal impact with antipersonnel fragmentation
Range Max.- 400m (437.6 yds)
Muzzle Velocity- 80mps (262fps)

DRACO (**D**irect-**R**ange **A**ir-**C**onsuming **O**rdnance) 40MM LV Multi-Purpose Grenade

The **DRACO** 40mm Low-Velocity Multi-Purpose Grenade is a fixed-type ammunition designed to be fired from a 40mm Grenade Launcher M79, M203 (attached to the M16/M16A1/M16A2 rifle) or Milkor MK-1. The round consists of an Enhanced Blast Explosive (EBX)-filled metal projectile body with a rotating band, a point initiating-base detonating fuze with Safe and Arm technology, and a cartridge-case assembly. Upon impact with the target, the firing pin is driven into the detonator, which in turn initiates the spit back charge, producing a jet which initiates the explosive train from the base forward, resulting in an armor-piercing jet of molten metal and fragmentation of the projectile body. With twice the fill amount of an M433, a 40% larger fragment pattern, and the Thermobaric effect of the EBX compound, the **DRACO** will provide superior performance against both Troops in the Open and MOUT-type engagements.

Figure B-21 DRACO

DRACO

Technical Information
Type- Enhanced Blast - Multi-Purpose
Fuze- SF801/M550
Charge- EBX
Body Material- Steel
Weight- 225 grams (90g YJO5)
Length- 120mm
Weapons- M79, M203, Milkor MK-1 launchers
Penetration- 65mm mild steel at normal impact with antipersonnel fragmentation
Range Max.- 400m (437.6 yds)
Muzzle Velocity- 80mps (262fps)

Appendix C – Night Vision Devices for M203

MOUNTING THE AN/PVS-4 (WITHOUT THE RAIL SYSTEM)

The operator must mount the AN/PVS-4 to the weapon before he zeroes it, and he must do both before he can qualify with the M203 grenade launcher. To mount the scope, the operator must
1. Remove the quadrant sight.
2. Position the mounting bracket assembly on the left side of the rifle so that the two clamps project through the opening under the handle. Loosen the wing nuts completely (Figure C-1).
3. Turn the clamp plates so that the pointed ends are in the UP position and are seated against the handle.
4. Tighten the wing nuts clockwise until the mounting bracket is secure against the weapon.
5. Position the sight in the groove on top of the bracket and align the threaded hole in the base of the sight-mounting adapter with the lever screw assembly. Tighten the screw clockwise firmly to secure the sight to the bracket.

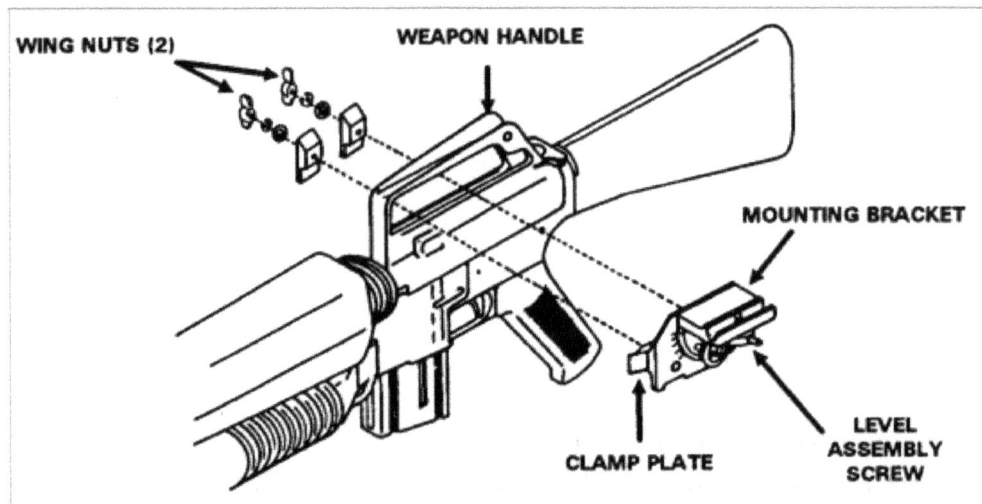

Figure C-1 Installing the mounting bracket

ZEROING THE AN/PVS-4 TO THE M203
After being mounted on the M203, the nightsight must be zeroed to the M16 before it can be zeroed to the M203. The M16 is then used to zero the nightsight to the M203. The grenade launcher rounds are fired only to confirm the zero. To zero the nightsight to the M203

1. **Center the Reticle Pattern**. Use the aiming points on the nightsight reticle (Figure C-2) and the range settings on the mounting bracket. Center the nightsight's reticle pattern within the field of view (FOV). Note that it may not

---

be centered even if it appears to be. To ensure it is, rotate the azimuth control knob either way until it stops. Then, rotate it back the opposite way; counting the number of clicks until it stops again (this may be any number of clicks between 200 and 600). Divide the number of clicks in half and rotate the knob in the original direction by that number of clicks. For example, if the total number of clicks is 500, rotate the knob back 250 clicks in the original direction. Center the elevation using the same procedure with the elevation control knob. The total amount of elevation clicks also varies between 200 and 600.

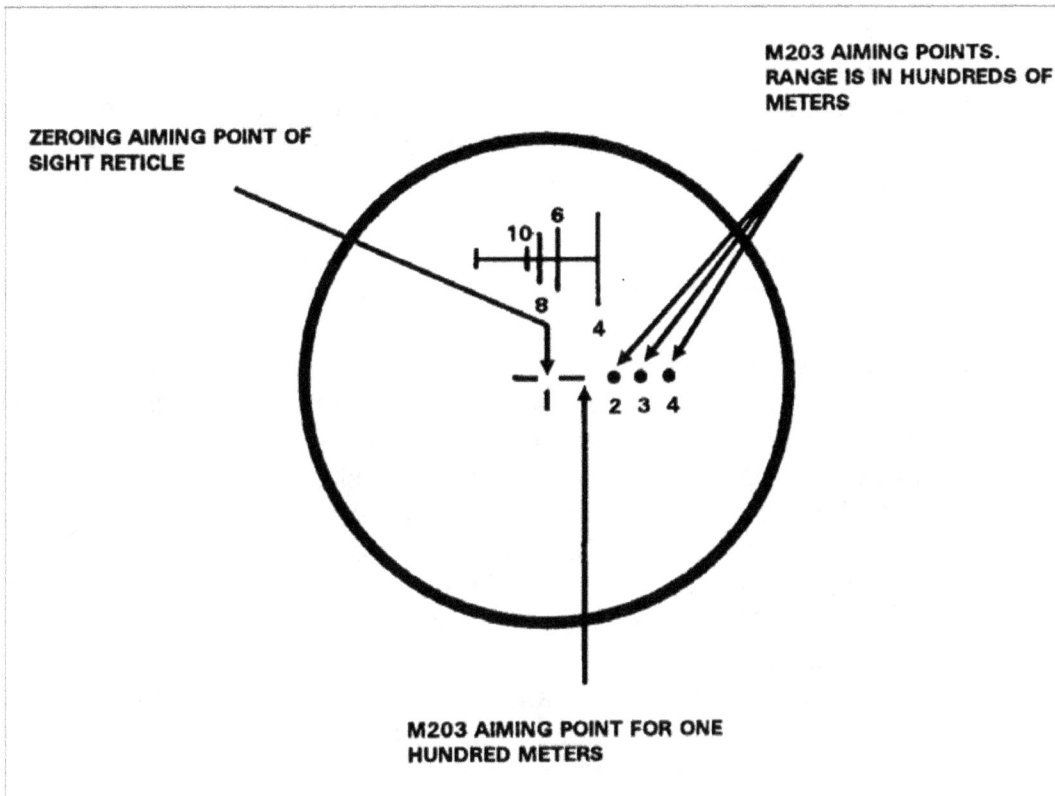

Figure C-2 Aiming points

2. **Adjust the Reticle Pattern**. Before adjusting the reticle pattern, the operator should fire three 5.56mm rounds and then retighten the mount wing nuts to securely seat the sight. Once this is done, the operator fires at a 10-meter target because hitting and spotting this target is easier than hitting a 25-meter target. This procedure may be performed in daylight using the daylight cover:

    A. Turn the sight on and adjust the reticle intensity to the desired level of illumination.

    B. Place an M16 25-meter target at 10 meters and stabilize the weapon.

    C. Fire a 5.56mm round at the center of the target and mark the hole the round makes.

    D. If the round misses the entire target, reseat the sight exactly as previously described.

E. If the round hits the target but not within 20 centimeters (8 inches) of the center, adjust the azimuth and elevation controls to bring the impact point toward the center of the target. Then fire a second round. Continue to fire single rounds and adjust the controls until the rounds strike within the desired distance from the center.

F. Once the reticle is adjusted, move the 25-meter target out to 25 meters and zero the grenade launcher. Do *not* remove the nightsight from the weapon until you have obtained a zero.

3. **Zero at 25 Meters**. This zero is not recorded. To obtain a 25-meter zero, the operator must

   A. Stabilize the weapon.
   B. Center the reticle's zeroing range aiming point on the target aiming point, which is in the center of the target (Figure C-3). Fire until you obtain a good three-round shot group. Triangulate and locate the center of the shot group.
   C. Even if the nightsight is dismounted and remounted on the same weapon, some changes in its zeroing will occur, so it must be zeroed again.
   D. Turn the azimuth and elevation control knobs to adjust the sight reticle. Move the center of the shot group 9.8 centimeters (3 7/8 inches) below and 4.2 centimeters (1 5/8 inches) to the right of the target aiming point. For example, if the shot group is high and to the left of the desired impact point, adjust the elevation down (DN) and the azimuth right (RT). One click of the azimuth or elevation adjustment moves the strike of the round .63 centimeter (1/4 inch) at a range of 25 meters. Two clicks move the reticle about one square on the target.
   E. After adjusting the reticle, assume a stable position. Place the reticle aiming point on the target aiming point and fire three more rounds.
   F. Repeat steps 3 and 4 until the rounds strike within a 3.2 centimeter (1 1/4 inches) circle in the desired location 9.8 centimeters (3 7/8 inches) below and 4.2 centimeters (1 5/8 inches) to the right of the aiming point, or until you have fired 12 rounds, whichever occurs first. If you are unable to zero the AN/PVS-4 after 12 rounds, the trainer must send you to remedial training.
   G. Confirm the zero on the grenade launcher range using a 200-meter target. Place the nightsight into operation and use its reticle, which has two parts. Use the vertical line in the upper part of the reticle to estimate range and the lower part to aim the weapon.
   H. Set the range as estimated on the range indicator of the mounting bracket.
   I. Engage the target, placing the aiming point of the sight reticle on the target's center of mass (Figure C-3). Fire the weapon using all your marksmanship skills. You have confirmed the zero if two of three rounds strike within 5 meters of the target.

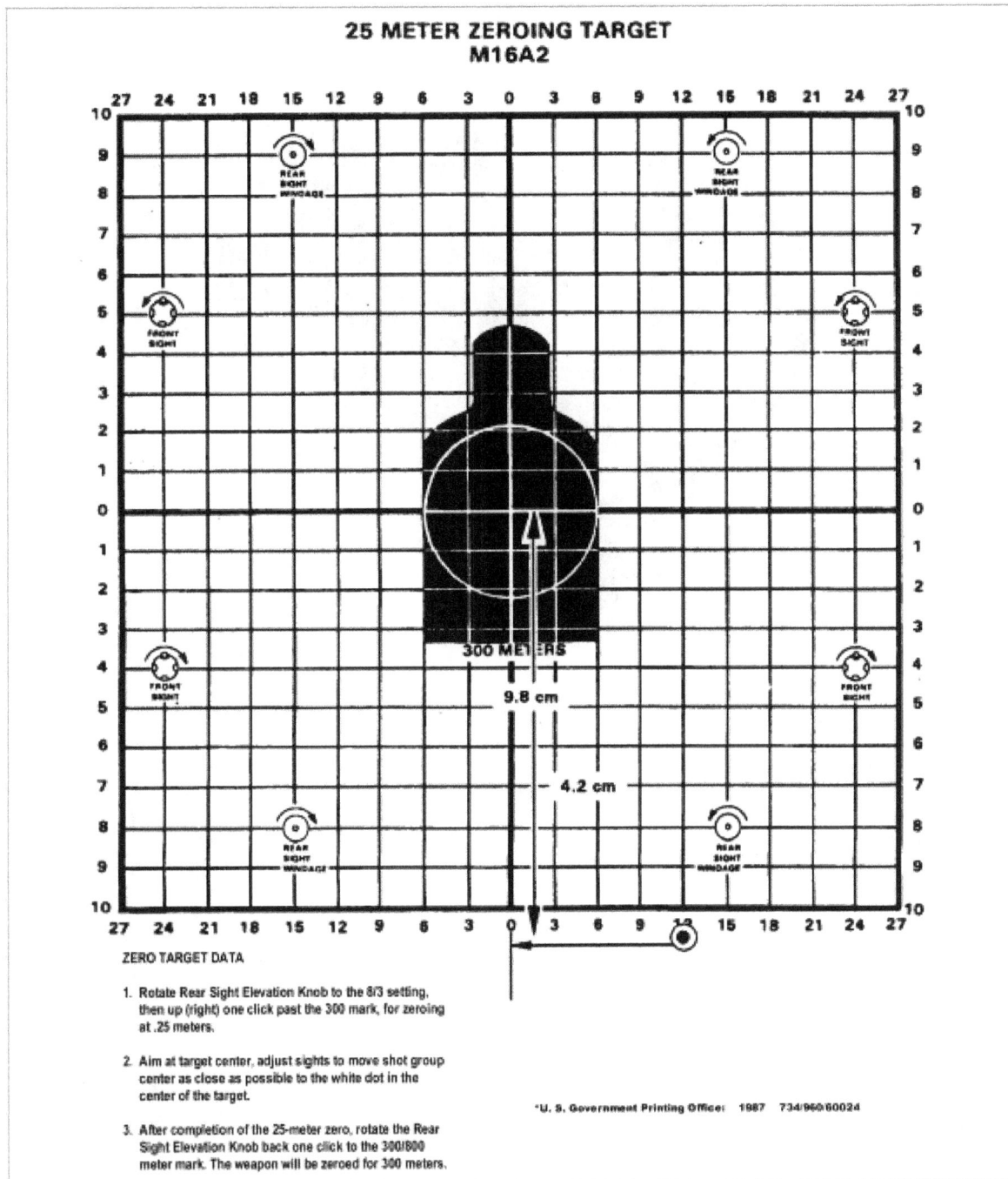

Figure C-3 Adjustment of rounds

AN/PSQ-18A-1 by Insight Technology

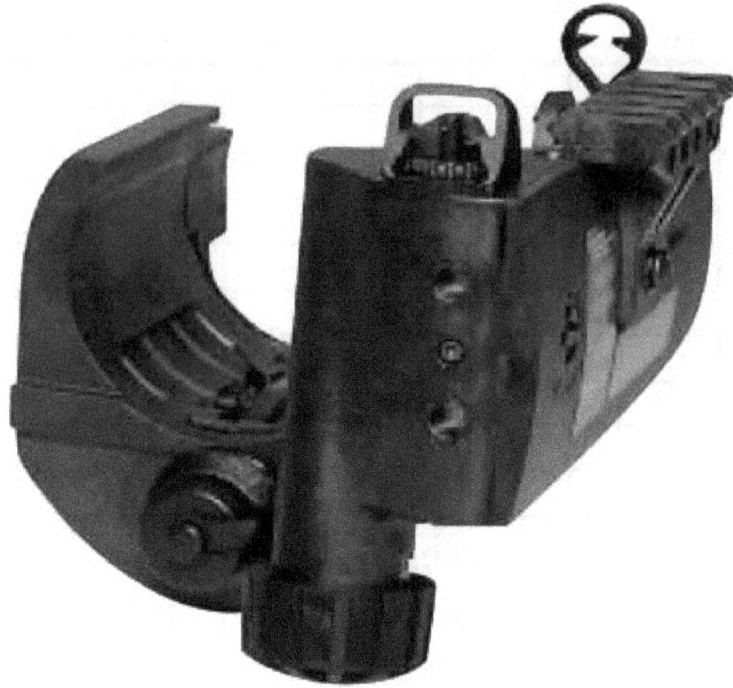

www.ingramcontent.com/pod-product-compliance
Lightning Source LLC
Chambersburg PA
CBHW080520110426
42742CB00017B/3180